ISRAEL IN REALITY

MULTICULTURAL DISCORD AND LOVE IN THE HOLY LAND

BY
Zvi November
M.A. (Anthropology)

For Molly and Moe, parents par excellence

Order this book online at www.trafford.com
or email orders@trafford.com

Most Trafford titles are also available at major online book retailers.

Print information available on the last page.

ISBN: 978-1-4251-6999-2 (sc)

Trafford rev. 12/21/2020

 www.trafford.com

North America & international
toll-free: 844-688-6899 (USA & Canada)
fax: 812 355 4082

ISRAEL IS PROBABLY THE MOST CONFUSING COUNTRY IN THE WORLD. Just about every aspect of life here is paradoxical. Israel is supposedly a Jewish country the way Thailand is Buddhist and Pakistan is Islamic. However, secularism prevails and most Israelis identify as Westerners in every way. Despite an ongoing Intifada (war) and the 2006 mini-war with the Lebanon-based Hizbullah guerilla army, the economy, led by the high tech sector, keeps growing by about 5% a year. On the other hand: corrupt politicians, pockets of poverty, plenty of crime, a deep rich-poor divide, strikes, scandals and governmental waste contribute to the impression that Israel is actually a Third World country in disguise.

Islamic terror organizations like Hamas and Islamic Jihad as well as the President of Iran are dedicated to the annihilation of the world's only Jewish state. Many European intellectuals, self-hating Jews and Israeli leftists think that Israel's creation (really re-creation) in 1948 was a mistake.

Israel is a nation at war but everyday life is quite peaceful despite the tension. This is a land that is literally in the East but belongs to the Western world. Life here may be stressful, but the talent to overcome obstacles and the drive to succeed is great.

Israel in Reality is an attempt to explain the inherent contradictions of a complex nation-state whose five or more component populations disagree on almost every issue. Based on my thirty-eight years inside the Israeli melting pot, this book offers unconventional insights into the existential problems Israelis wrestle with every day.

CONTENTS

INTRODUCTION

EVERY SO OFTEN I VISIT THE US OR ENTERTAIN GUESTS FROM EUROPE. My friends invariably ask me many questions about Israel. "Are you religious?" "Do you earn enough money to live on?" "Who did you vote for and why?" "Why did you disengage from Gaza without some sort of agreement?" "What are you going to do about Hamas?" "What does the future hold for you?" I take these questions very personally because the pronoun "you" appears in all of them. My answers, of course, are based on my experiences and observations of living in Israel thirty-eight years. My responses, furthermore, are never simple since almost all of Israel's dilemmas are paradoxical and, or multi-faceted. How, for instance, should the state relate to its Arab citizens (comprising some 20% of the population) when so many of them identify with the Arab side in the Arab-Israeli conflict and constantly complain about alleged discrimination?

My explanations almost always combine both macro and micro level facts. For example, Arab workmen add balconies on to my apartment building so my religious neighbors can construct traditional booths to celebrate the Succoth holiday properly. These workmen may well be donating part of their wages to the Islamic Jihad organization that rejects all peace overtures and perpetrates terrorist atrocities against Israelis. On the macro level, the Arab world still maintains a boycott of Israeli manufactured goods but the local shuks (open-air markets) here are full of Arab-grown produce that people buy; some enthusiastically and some reluctantly. I would guess that half of the shuk hawkers and supermarket personnel are Arabs.

I also believe that it is important to add an intercultural perspective to my answers because Israel is totally immersed in the global economy and subject to extensive international scrutiny. The majority of Israelis have roots in countries such as Poland, Russia, France, Argentina, Morocco and Iran. Israelis also enjoy traveling abroad frequently to take a respite from their tiny land full of nervous tension surrounded by belligerent neighbors. Israelis feel that they have to break away from their isolation every once in a while by touring overseas for pleasure, visiting relatives, attending conferences, participating in trade fairs and cementing business agreements with foreign firms.

Israelis have a dual relationship with the rest of the world. On the tourism level, Western Europe and America are pleasant and hospitable lands where Israelis enjoy interacting with the local folks. On the political level, many Israelis feel that, 'the whole world is against us'. Most Islamic countries reject Israel's right to exist. British unions threaten Israel with boycotts, a French diplomat calls Israel "a shitty little country" and the UN is preoccupied with condemning Israel at every opportunity.

In truth, Israelis have both friends and foes around the globe. Israel's situation is not as unique as some people think. Other countries face equally serious threats. Sri Lanka, for example, is an island paradise torn by inter-ethnic strife for the last thirty years or more. In terms of victims and damage, the terror war in Sri Lanka is probably worse than the Arab-Israeli struggle. There are also similarities to Taiwan's situation as a country shunned by many states but determined not to be taken over by mainland China.

Americans get their news from CNN, Fox, *The New York Times* and other outlets which draw criticism from watchdog groups such as Camera, Honestreporting and Eye on the Post [*Washington Post*] because of slanted reporting and commentaries. The BBC, as Melanie Phillips and other British observers regularly demonstrate, is completely one-sided. It portrays the Palestinians as angels and the Israelis as villains. Even when Palestinians kidnapped BBC reporter Alan Johnston and held him captive for a few months in Gaza, the BBC continued to be sympathetic to the Palestinians. What would have been the BBC's reaction had Johnston been taken by Israelis? Upon leaving Gaza, Johnston's press conference along side Hamas chiefs seemed like a happy birthday party. According to a radio news item I heard on 26 July 2007, a month after Johnston's release, it appears that Gordon Brown's government is now exploring ways to work with the Hamas leadership despite its firm Islamic terror credentials.

The media in Israel determines the national agenda and no wise politician or civil servant would dare tackle this omnipotent oligarchy. Given both Israeli and international media distortions of what transpires in Israel, I feel compelled to set the record straight. I know from personal experience that the media's "truth" and the actual facts on the ground do not normally coincide. This is my major impetus for writing about Israel's intra-societal dissonance and chaos (*balagan* in colloquial Hebrew). Israeli society is like a knotted ball of string that is difficult to unravel.

Israel is full of nervous energy and nervous tension; discharged by people working hard. But many tensions derive from the contradictions inherent in the state itself. Some Israelis want Israel to be a Jewish state in which education, government, law and culture radiate an unmistakable Jewish character. Others envision Israel as a refuge for Jews; a safe haven wherein a Jew can observe or not observe Judaism in any way he or she sees fit. The 1948 Declaration of Independence affirms that Israel is a **Jewish** as well as **democratic** state that grants full equality to all its citizens including ethnic minorities. The Supreme Court, the intellectual elite and media commanders always stress <u>democracy</u> whenever there is a conflict between what seems like elementary human rights and the customs of traditional Judaism. A simple illustration of this clash concerns marriage. Should an Israeli be free to marry anyone he or she desires or is he restricted to a Jewish partner as called for in traditional Jewish law? If the Druze minority is obligated to serve in the army, why shouldn't Arab citizens be drafted as well if they demand equal treatment in other spheres?

The separation of church and state is a fundamental principle in the West. The US is considered by many to be the most successful multi-cultural society in the world because it largely adheres to this doctrine. By contrast, a great many other nations are defined by their religious-ethnic essence. Thailand is a Buddhist country with a constitutional monarch who is treated as a demigod. Over fifty countries around the world swear allegiance to the Koran and proclaim that the laws of Islam determine their social realities. Homogeneous Japan has, until now, done its utmost to preserve its pure Japanese character. Even third generation Koreans born and raised in Japan are not yet fully accepted into Japanese society.

Israel is the world's only Jewish state. A comedian once remarked that if someone were to set up another Jewish state, he would be the first to move there. Another funny man defined

Israel as the 'best Arab state in the world'. A small minority of Israelis who have distanced themselves from Judaism advocate 'a state for all its citizens', which, in all its ramifications, would mean the end of Israel as a Jewish state.

To help prevent such an eventuality, *Efrat* (www.efrat.org.il), a not-for-profit organization whose objective is to encourage and financially support increased Jewish fertility does outreach work. It provides poor families with the gear and food needed to care for newborn children. *Efrat* discourages abortions (of which there are about 20,000 each year) and extends assistance to pregnant women contemplating abortions.

I belong to secular Israel but unlike most of my non-religious countrymen I recognize the supreme centrality of Jewish religious practice. Before it became a political movement, Zionism was, and still is, an important tenant of Judaism. The Land of Israel plays a major role in Jewish aspirations. The Jews are a nation because they have a unique land and culture of their own. The Jewish religion is at the very center of this culture. Deleting the Jewish religion from Jewish ethnicity inevitably leads to assimilation and national self-destruction. Therefore, even though I am not myself religious, I believe that it is crucial to enhance Israel's Jewish character by doing everything possible to strengthen Jewish education and culture (which includes Hebrew literature) and develop an updated accommodation with religious traditions.

To buttress Israeli society today, one has to remember that Jewish communal life in the Diaspora over the past two millennia was centered on the synagogue. Jews perpetuated their culture by obstinately adhering to their own religious rituals, most of which take place in the synagogue. Educational activities, charitable work and the resolution of quarrels were also, as a rule, focused on the synagogue and the community's rabbi. This facet of traditional Judaism has an important role to play in Israel today. Furthermore, when relating to Jewish national survival over the past two thousand years one also has to tackle the phenomenon of anti-Semitism.

Jew-hating has taken many diverse formats in different places. In Poland the Jews suffered severe abuse because, it was claimed, they insisted on dressing, eating and acting differently. But in late

19th century Germany, by contrast, Jews were despised because they aped their German neighbors in dress and manners. Jews did everything in their power to be Germans. Apropos of the urge to assimilate, I once saw a reprinted British National Front cartoon in London's venerable *Jewish Chronicle*. A stout man on a podium declares that, 'we must be tolerant of blacks and other minorities' and someone in the crowd yells back, 'that's right, Mr. Cohen'. Jews are often accused of undermining national interests, even in liberal democracies where they have successfully assimilated.

Today, Israel bashing is a modern form of anti-Semitism. A cornerstone of the foreign policies of many nations such as Malaysia, Pakistan, Iran, South Africa and, more recently, Venezuela, to mention just a few, demands dangerous concessions from Israel or its outright destruction.

We cannot leave the subject of anti-Semitism without relating to the activities of self-hating Jews. Karl Marx was an ardent anti-Semite. He attacked the bourgeoisie and Jews which, in his estimation, were one and the same. The number of Jew-hating Jews (almost exclusively identified with the Left) is large. In Israel, too, some Israeli professors have revised Israeli history so as to blame the Zionist side for the Israeli-Arab conflict. Kenneth Levin provides a detailed synopsis of the writings and activities of these Jewish anti-Semites in his *The Oslo Syndrome, Delusions of a People Under Siege*. Levin points out that these self-hating Israelis are the direct descendents of Jewish apostates who deserted the Jewish people throughout its long history.

Psychiatry professor Sander Gilman in his monograph *Jewish Self-Hatred* (1986) examines, in great detail, both Jewish and gentile literature of the 19th and 20th centuries as well as intellectual thought as they pertain to alleged Jewish physical and mental inferiority. Jews (like blacks and homosexuals in other contexts) who lived in Germany and other Western societies that believed in their inherent perverted or aberrant nature accepted these "truths" in their own minds and became self-haters. Many of those Jews who converted to Christianity to escape, as it were, their own inferior status, became avid anti-Semites themselves. However, the gentile world into which they were so eager to integrate themselves was quite cognizant of these maneuvers and never fully accepted Baptized Jews as the history of Germany, before and after the Nazi takeover, confirms. Gilman discusses the double bind wherein Jews are not accepted for what they are nor can they successfully escape this predicament by imitating their Christian neighbors. This paradoxical condition seems to have re-emerged in Israel where the hunger for peace manifests itself in a craving for acceptance in the Middle East.

Arieh Stav is the director of The Ariel Center for Policy Research. In 1998 he authored Policy Paper No. 22, "*The Dialectic of Self-Hatred in Israel*". The following is a quote from page 13 because we cannot fully understand Israel without taking note of Israeli anti-Semitism:

> "*One ought to bear in mind that Zionism is simply nationalism, just as "Englishness" is the nationalism of the English and "Frenchism" is the nationalism of the French or Arabism ('Uruba'), the nationalism of the Arabs, for that matter. Casting derision on Zionism therefore means negating Jewish nationalism which is nothing other than committing national suicide. The lethal mockery called the "peace process", whereby Zionism is programmed to lose the reason for its physical and spiritual existence, is the default option of Jewish radicalism, which seeks to restore the health of an expiring leftism.*
>
> *Since the Left possesses intellectual hegemony over the elites that shape the mental world of Israel's secularists, the browbeaten public yields, its brains battered with the orgy of peace, surrendering to the slow-killing drug in which yearnings and delusion have combined with the unique Jewish ability for pathological self-deception when in the role of victim.*"

This short survey is my attempt to fit most of the puzzle pieces together into a description of Israeli society as an organic whole whose many parts, unfortunately, don't work very well together. There is, however, every reason to believe that Israeli optimism and vibrancy will triumph in the end. On balance, living in Israel is a positive experience. The society is free; the people are friendly, intellectually honest and dedicated to peace, although there are serious disagreements on how to achieve it. As the old WWII song in Britain declared, 'you've got to look on the bright side' of everything.

1
POTENTIALLY THE GREATEST
COUNTRY IN THE WORLD

When I was a teen-ager growing up in the US during the optimistic 1950s a catchy TV jingle went as follows: "See the USA in your Chevrolet, America is the greatest land of all". Having lived in six other countries I now know that there are other outstanding places on our planet. I also know that Israel has the potential to join top-rated nations like Sweden and Switzerland. Indeed, Israelis often cite Switzerland as a model to be emulated.

If Israel were not constantly harassed by its Arab enemies, it would probably take first place in the 200 plus living-standard categories that are used to determine the quality of life I would like to enjoy. Israel could easily become another Switzerland if it were not subject to nerve-racking external pressures from Arab and Islamic forces and internal fissures that undermine its self-confidence and social solidarity.

Israel's greatest asset is its people. An egalitarian ethos combined with a big dose of common sense and the expectation that men and (to a lesser extent) women at work should take the initiative characterizes the labor force. This pretty much describes kibbutz and moshav village farm workers who plow the fields and fill the markets with huge quantities of fresh fruits and vegetables all year round. Tourists are whisked through Jerusalem's Machene Yehuda open air market where they are overwhelmed by the abundance. In addition to ordinary apples, pears, oranges, etc., tropical fruits such as bananas, avocados and mangos are available at low prices because they are grown locally in a country the size of New Jersey. All these health-giving delicacies are sold by the kilo. Lately, my wife has converted our household to organic produce that are equally plentiful. Now the fruits and vegetables we eat are chemical-free.

There are several agricultural research centers but the Volcani Institute near Rishon LeZion is the premier center that literally invents new varieties of fruits and vegetables. Today it is concentrating on bringing back the true tastes of produce that have lost their natural flavors due to synthetic commercial agricultural practices. Even though Israel's ever-expanding urban population means that farmlands near cities and towns are constantly being converted into housing developments, Israel continues to export citrus, avocados, flowers and other fresh produce to Europe. Agrexco is the main export company that ships fresh farm produce to consumers abroad to earn cash to pay for imported delicacies and status items like Volvos and Red Label whiskey.

Another food branch that has been successfully developed is fish farming both in sweet water ponds and ocean cages. Many varieties from all over the world have been adapted to Israeli conditions. Environmentalists claimed that fish raised in the Gulf of Eilat led to a decrease in wild fish reproduction and the decimation of coral formations. However, a biologist friend of mine conducted research over several years. He found that this assertion, although politically correct, was, in light of his data, really false.

In addition to abundant quantities of fish, Israelis are also awash in dairy products. The Israeli Frisian cow (a cross between the native cow and the Dutch Frisian) holds world records for milk production. Consumers who are critical of bovine-derived milk can buy sheep and goat milk cheese and yogurt, which some nutritionists consider superior, in any supermarket.

Meat is available all the time since cows, sheep, chickens and turkeys are raised in large numbers. Non-kosher meats as well as shrimp and other proscribed foods, that according to Jewish law are taboo, are a source of contention between observant and non-observant Jews. However, several hundred thousand non-Jews (mainly from Eastern Europe) and individuals like Tommy Lapid, a famous journalist and one time member of the Knesset who also served as justice minister, feel that their rights are restricted by government enforced kashrus (kosher) regulations. These people, nevertheless, can find all the proscribed food items they relish in markets that cater to foreigners and in many restaurants as well. Observant Jews who eat only kosher food have access to thousands of restaurants that are inspected by *mashgichim*, kashrus inspectors. Almost every hotel, even kibbutz guest houses, along with the majority of restaurants display certificates confirming that the fare they serve is absolutely kosher. Of course, visitors and locals alike have a wide choice of cuisine styles ranging from sushi to spaghetti to the ever-popular delicacies from all over the Mediterranean basin, in kosher or non-kosher formats. In short, Israel has evolved into a gourmet's paradise. Even Israeli wines have won prizes for their quality in France. And *The Book of New Israel Food* by Janna Gur (www.tasteofisrael.com) details Israel's coming of age in culinary matters.

The Israeli buffet breakfast served by hotels is justly famous. A huge variety of morning foods goes on display and you are invited to eat as much as you can. This mode of hospitality reflects, I believe, the Israeli habit of eating frequently. People snack in the street, on buses and at their office desks. Most government offices and large companies operate cafeterias. Smaller offices have kiosks that serve light meals and provide room service to busy clerks. I often participated in meetings that automatically included refreshments.

When not at work, Israelis patronize the ubiquitous sidewalk cafes. Downtown Jerusalem as well as all city centers has innumerable café-restaurants where people, very much like their European counterparts, consume tea, coffee, cakes, falafel, humus, techina and shwarma. In view of its success a leading café chain, *Aroma* has begun opening branches in the US to compete with *Starbucks*.

As in Europe, famous chefs have their own TV shows that my wife greatly enjoys.

Jewish leaders of almost every persuasion are very worried about assimilation and the future of the Jewish nation. Demographic studies reveal that most Jewish communities around the world have low birth rates and suffer from high levels of intermarriage between Jews and gentiles. Whereas Diaspora communities are decreasing in size, Israeli society exhibits much more vitality and is now the paramount mainspring reinforcing Jewish religion, national consciousness and culture. Many organizations like Young Judea, WUJS (World Union of Jewish Students) as well as the Hebrew University and other institutions of higher education run myriad programs of study for overseas students in English, Spanish and French. Students can learn Hebrew in most of these programs and at special *ulpans* (seminars that specialize in language instruction). One can also study Arabic and Islamic culture on an equally high level because Israeli universities have excellent Middle East studies departments. Some of the world's leading Islamic scholars like Bernard Lewis and Bat Ye'or are Jewish.

In June, 2006 Gu Yi, a twenty-one year old Chinese e-mail pen pal of mine visited Israel for the first time. Gu Yi was raised in Shanghai but studied Hebrew, Jewish studies and Middle Eastern affairs at Beijing University. He spent some five weeks at the Hebrew University which he enjoyed immensely. The fact is that there is an impressive number of East Asians studying at Israeli universities all year round.

The Makuya Center is less than a kilometer from my house. This Japanese Christian group believes that to be better Christians, they have to study Hebrew, the Bible and Christianity's Jewish roots at their source. Every March, a large troupe of Makuya strolls through downtown Jerusalem waving Japanese and Israeli flags and spreading much good will. Similarly, Christian Koreans and Finns maintain permanent offices in Jerusalem to assist pilgrims from their respective countries. The International Christian Embassy in Jerusalem is very active. The ICEJ extends aid to needy people (e.g. older non-Jewish immigrants from the former USSR), operates a daily Internet news service, generally promotes Israeli interests and organizes a yearly Tabernacle festival for thousands of participants from around the world every year at Succoth. An equally dedicated group is the International Fellowship of Christians and Jews under the direction of Rabbi Yechiel Eckstein. The Fellowship has raised and contributed millions of dollars to help build shelters in Sderot, a city under constant Kassam rocket bombardment. A smaller group called *Ohavei Zion* (Lovers of Zion) with headquarters in Jaffa also appears on the streets to express Christian solidarity with ordinary Israelis. All this is in addition to several Christian villages run by church groups intent on making a positive contribution to Israel.

Both Jews and gentiles from all over the world visit Israel as tourists or short-term students or attend conferences here. Many of these people are sympathetic to Israel's plight and feel they want to express their support, especially when tensions rise. A trip to Israel, therefore, is often more than simply a tourism experience. It can also prove to be a deep spiritual encounter, something that one does not find in Hawaii. Occasionally, travelers get a bit carried away by the holiness they feel or think they feel. Every once in a while I see long-bearded men in flowing robes as well as women attired in biblical costume in the center of town on Ben-Yehuda street preaching at the top of their lungs in an effort to redeem sinners. Some of these individuals suffer from what has become known as the "Jerusalem Syndrome", a condition wherein one identifies with Jesus or some other biblical figure.

One of the Arabs' main complaints against Israel is that it is an artificial country imposed on the Levant by Europeans out of a sense of guilt deriving from the Holocaust. The truth, however, is that world Jewry started re-building the Jewish state in the 19th century, long before WWII. Wealthy Jews purchased large tracts of land before 1900 and agricultural towns like Zichron Ya'akov were established on these holdings. The Hebrew University with financial support from abroad was dedicated in 1925. Walk down any university campus in Israel and you will see that each building bears the name of the family that donated the money to construct it. On the walls of the two large Hadassah hospitals in Jerusalem (founded by Henrietta Szold before WWI) one can see the names of thousands of contributors, primarily from the US, because the

Hadassah organization is the American version of the women's international Zionist movement (WIZO). The magnificent Lerner Sports Center where I work out is a multi-million dollar gift from Washington, D.C.'s highly respected and generous Annette and Theodore Lerner family. The architecturally esteemed Supreme Court building is a gift from the Rothchilds. The Safras, a wealthy Lebanese Jewish banking family, provided much of the funds that were used to create the lovely Jerusalem municipal compound.

These are just a few examples of thousands of similar philanthropic projects that can be found everywhere. When overseas Jews visit, they feel that they have come home and express themselves in the first person; 'What a wonderful country **we** have built!' Many other nationalities (e.g. the Chinese, Greeks, Italians, Copts and Armenians) also feel a deep sense of attachment to their homelands but the Jewish love for the Land of Israel is exceptionally strong. Someone once commented that world Jewry's support of Israel is, in effect, a self-imposed tax. I recently attended a lecture by the former Chief Rabbi, Israel Lau, who noted that many foreign nations have conquered the Land of Israel but only the Jews love it passionately and express this love by building it up and constantly introducing improvements. And Arabs, as hospital patients, university students and sports enthusiasts, have equal access to all these modern amenities.

Israel also reaches out to the world. One of my first counselor jobs was with the Ministry of Agriculture's Foreign Training Department. I coordinated the social activities of trainees from the Philippines, Iran (before the Islamic revolution), Cambodia, Thailand and several African countries who studied advanced animal husbandry and agriculture. Today, the government's Volcani Institute has a similar international program that focuses on genetic research and plant improvement. For decades, the Foreign Ministry has run a variety of training courses for men and women from developing nations. All this is in addition to the many university cooperation programs and medical assistance missions sent to afflicted areas in Africa and other Third World locations.

Quite a few Israeli intellectuals (in addition to those who have been awarded Nobel Prizes) have gained international recognition. For example, Professor Uri Epstein of the Hebrew University received the Japanese Emperor's award for his work on Japanese musicology. A second Hebrew University professor, Ben Ami Shiloni is an acknowledged expert on Japan who wrote a fascinating book that draws surprising parallels between the Jews and the Japanese.

It is an understatement to say that Israel is colorful and cosmopolitan. Italian priests lead pilgrim groups to Christianity's holiest churches. They can find accommodations in hotels and monasteries. The Dalai Lhama has visited several times. He is always welcome in Israel and supported by Israeli Friends of the Tibetan People, a group that annoys the Chinese Embassy. World class scholars are frequently official guests who deliver lectures open to the public. Martin Gilbert, Churchill's biographer, delivered an extraordinary presentation about Jewish fortitude through the ages at the 23rd biennial International Book Fair in Jerusalem in February, 2007.

Most European countries operate cultural centers and libraries in the big cities. Additionally, they sponsor visits of top-flight musicians and other artists from their respective nations in addition to film fairs.

There are well-known medieval maps that place Jerusalem at the center of the world. As a Jerusalem resident, I have come to feel that this city really has become pivotal for much that is evolving in our precarious world. There are thousands of foreign journalists assigned to cover Israel and the Arab conflict. Many of them reside in Jerusalem. The amount of media scrutiny that Israel attracts is far in excess of the attention paid to comparable countries like Denmark, Belgium or New Zealand.

Natural amenities are taken for granted. The weather is usually perfect even though a summer heat wave (called *chamsin*) can sap one's energy. On the other hand, winters are mild and storms infrequent in this sub-tropic, semi-arid land of milk and honey. With a long coastline, there are plenty of beaches and shore resorts. Marinas now harbor yachts and water sports are popular. Israel has highly competitive sailors and surf boarders.

Being a hot country, air conditioning is standard in buildings and vehicles. Unfortunately, as a dry country, Israel has a serious water supply problem. Parenthetically, I once read a book which predicts that future wars in the Middle East will be over securing water sources. When I first arrived in 1969 I was informed that Israel, back then, 'uses about 97% of its water resources'. Today the population has doubled to over seven million but we still miraculously have enough water. Nevertheless, water experts appear on TV every so often to warn the public about an impending water shortage. Indeed, the World Bank is very worried about the increasing scarcity of water throughout the Arab Middle East.

Mekorot is the government company that manages Israel's water resources; supplying about one and a half billion cubic meters of water every year. The company maintains over 10,000 kilometers of pipe lines. Furthermore, Mekorot's waste water recycling and desalinization operations are large-scale activities that significantly supplement water reserves.

A desalinization plant near Ashkelon adds some 50 million cubic meters a year to the national water grid. In 2007, a second desalinization plant was opened. But the 1994 peace treaty with Jordan includes a clause that obligates Israel to provide Jordan with 50 million cubic meters annually from the Jordan River. Almost every drop of water exiting the Kinneret Lake heading for the Dead Sea is now in use. The trickle of water reaching the Dead Sea is insufficient to maintain the Sea's level so its shore line keeps receding. At one spa, a golf cart now takes bathers to the distant beach. A plan to solve this problem entails digging a canal from the Red Sea down to the Dead Sea. However, environmentalists are already demanding detailed evaluations of possible damage before Israeli-Jordanian construction begins.

As in the rest of the developed world, bottled spring water has become popular and water filter companies do a brisk business. Be that as it may, it is perfectly safe to drink tap water which contains both chlorine and fluoride and whose mineral content is about thirty parts per million. This contrasts with about 3 ppm in the US. While Israelis learn to conserve water at an early age, they are also accustomed to having easy access to swimming pools. Most Israelis take showers. Filling up a bath tub, as is or was customary in England, is an extravagance that does not fit into Israeli living conditions.

ISRAEL IN REALITY

Israel is a free-wheeling, dynamic country full of interesting people. With a liberalized economy, foreign executives like doing business in Tel Aviv whose stock exchange indexes keep going up. While traveling in the US in 2006 I met a computer engineer on a flight. This Hong Kong born Chinese fellow told me that his employer, Intel, sends him to Israel several times a year and he loves the country. In a similar positive vane, a June 22, 2007 newspaper report quoted Leo Apotheker, the SAP AG Company's CEO who employs 850 workers in Israel at two research facilities. Apotheker announced that he was fully satisfied with his Israeli research units and would not contemplate closing them.

The international media and especially the pro-Palestinian, biased BBC paint a dismal picture of Israel which, when analyzed objectively, proves false. We are led to forget that Israel and the Jews have many good friends who support Israel because they know that this country is an open, moral society; full of challenges and plenty of excitement. Despite all its enormous problems and the continuous Arab/Islamic onslaught, Israel is a great place to live. The daily struggle to succeed in an unpredictable environment is invigorating and generates a high level of personal satisfaction.

2
FINDING THE GROOVES

I moved to Israel from the U.S. in 1969. The Hebrew term for such a life-altering event is *aliya*, literally *going up* to the Promised Land. I arrived independently but the Jewish Agency and many other non-profit organizations operate abroad to encourage and assist new immigrants, known as *olim*, to emigrate and integrate successfully. Getting settled, however, can prove difficult because one has to learn the language, find employment and housing, enroll the kids in school and get acquainted with an unfamiliar culture.

I was determined to learn Hebrew as quickly as possible. To realize this goal, I had to insist on speaking Hebrew with everyone I met. Most Israelis can carry on rudimentary conversations in English and they enjoy nothing better than practicing their English with Americans. Had I acceded to their wish, it would have taken much longer to achieve fluency.

Since I landed as a single adult, I was quite flexible in terms of employment. At the very onset I settled into a kibbutz (collective settlement) near Beer Sheva as a volunteer worker. For many decades large numbers of young Europeans and some Americans eagerly worked on kibbutzim where they received bed and board and sometimes Hebrew lessons in exchange for their labor. I was assigned to a modest factory that produces drip irrigation hoses and fittings. These products are in great demand in many arid countries as well as the dryer parts of China.

About three months later I spotted an ad for an English teacher on a small kibbutz near the Kinneret Lake. I went for an interview and got the job. I was given a choice of receiving a monthly salary and paying the kibbutz for my room and board or working as a volunteer. I chose the latter to signify my desire to feel part of the extended kibbutz family and immediately moved north to take up my new post. This small kibbutz was strictly agricultural and relatively poor. Its poverty was revealed in the communal dining room where the quantity of food served was less than at my first kibbutz which was larger and far more prosperous. The first kibbutz, Chatzerim, grew wheat, had peach orchards, raised dairy cows and chickens and harvested Egyptian variety cotton in addition to the successful plastic irrigation equipment factory.

On Chukuk, the second kibbutz, I taught English to ten- and eleven-year-olds about half of whom were actually city children that the welfare service had taken from problematic families in nearby towns. These city kids were assigned to kibbutz families that filled the role of foster parents. Generally, children like living on kibbutzim where they enjoy a great deal of freedom and have many friends their own age.

Later, I left this isolated kibbutz when I met the director of the Kiryat Shmona community center. Community centers, known by their Hebrew acronym *matnasim*, play an important role, especially in smaller towns, because they offer classes in everything from music and crafts to karate, organize athletic activities and provide facilities for social activities. The director invited me to stay with him for a week. He wanted to add me to his staff as an outreach worker but the position never materialized. During that week I acquainted myself with the town's neighborhoods and social problems while the director met several times with the mayor who was *not* willing to put me on *his* payroll. The mayor agreed to have me as a community worker but only if my salary came out of someone else's budget.

Israel is a highly centralized state. Local budgets are, to a great extent, allocated from Jerusalem. Local governments receive these funds over which they are given control and use them at their discretion. Mayors, especially in small towns like Kiryat Shmona, have a lot of power because they control a cash flow which originates at the national treasury. The way they dispense these public monies reflects their personal political priorities. Recently, a number of municipal employees have not been paid for months as a result of financial mismanagement. This problem is especially acute in Arab municipalities where traditional clan solidarity often overrides principles of equality and good government whose actions are open to public scrutiny and criticism.

Although I never got to work in Kiryat Shmona, I did find a place on the 1971 Tel Dan archaeological excavation just fifteen minutes away by bus. Back then, volunteers like me enthusiastically dug up precious artifacts in exchange for room and board. I believe that I had a good deal because I am an archaeology buff and the thrill of unearthing a 3000 year old city wall is tremendously exciting. I also got to befriend many members of the Israel Antiquities Department, later re-organized as the Antiquities Authority. Today, excavation volunteers have to pay the Antiquities Authority or university research team doing the digging. After all, participating in a dig is a valuable learning experience and you are also provided with food and sleeping accommodations.

During the 1970s I landed several jobs as a guidance counselor. Taking care of adolescents in dormitory situations is ideal for single people but teen-agers can literally drive you crazy. I once found myself coaxing a sixteen year old boy back into the third floor dorm from his perch outside of his room's window. Occasionally I had to retrieve a bunch of kids from their favorite night club at 2:00 a.m. The boys needed me on the basketball court. The girls enjoyed teasing me. I worked 24 hours a day.

In another counselor post, I served as a role model cum policeman for American college kids whose wealthy grandparents had shipped them off to Israel where it was hoped they would "straighten out". These youngsters were doing drugs and staying up all night "discovering themselves". It was during that school year that I learned all about the generation gap that had not as yet taken root in Israel.

As the years passed I became more Israeli and found other jobs with somewhat better conditions. At one point I was accepted by the Welfare Ministry as an adult probation officer even though I do not have social worker credentials. The Probation Service is staffed overwhelmingly by female social workers who have been taught to see crime (i.e. violence, theft and burglary) as social ills of an imperfect society. Young men convicted of felonies have to first be understood and then reformed through heart to heart weekly dialogues. I observed that many of the female officers were quite sensitive to their clients' predicaments and assumed a protective role vis-à-vis the courts and police.

At one juncture, in 1977, I visited the Jerusalem Chamber of Commerce. I asked them what kind of business undertaking has good potential and the straightforward response was, "open a restaurant". Since I had had little business experience, I decided to explore other opportunities. Eventually I was accepted by the government Employment Service as a job placement counselor. I worked for the Employment Service for twenty-four years; developing an in-depth knowledge of the job market and retraining programs.

At that time, Israeli labor law, with certain exceptions, obliged employers to hire their workers exclusively through local government labor exchanges. The idea behind this system was to enable the government to regulate access to employment along the guidelines it set. This arrangement fell between the more or less free, open job market in the US and job allocations in the former Soviet Union. In the USSR, Russian high school as well as college graduates were assigned to factories and offices whether they were needed there or not. Back then in the communist USSR there were no government labor exchanges because, theoretically, there was no need for them. But Israel has official labor exchanges all over the country. Employers call in job openings and the labor exchange clerks send them candidates from the unemployed clientele, most of whom are drawing unemployment compensation. Unfortunately, this system does not work very well for several reasons. The main problem is that people want 'good' jobs which, as many studies show, are rarely advertised nor listed in the labor exchanges. Furthermore, unemployment payments can be as high as 76% of one's previous gross wages. Individuals receiving unemployment benefits can refuse jobs that pay less than their unemployment compensation.

Nowadays, private temporary employment agencies such as *Manpower* control a large percentage of the available jobs. In Israel, employers pay their fees as it is against the law for them to charge job seekers. Because of the many laws that obligate employers to pay for vacation time, sick leave and severance pay, many companies prefer to avoid the employer-employee relationship by passing it on to one of the private manpower agencies.

It is generally recognized that the most effective way to get a good job, as in many other countries, is to use your *proteksia*; apply the principle of 'it's who you know and not what you know'. Getting a job in the electric or telephone company or one of the hundreds of government companies is often a question of the right connections. This also holds true for the civil service itself which is by far Israel's largest employer. Most of my colleagues at the Labor Exchange got their jobs through connections to political activists who could promote their placement using the age-old technique of 'one hand washing the other'. These same people also used their patrons to help them climb the bureaucratic ladder regardless of their talents. "Sewn up" was the term used when a favored insider was about to get promoted to a higher position in the bureaucracy.

Just being an ordinary worker in a shop is not a preferred option. If you are going to be a plumber, carpenter or painter, you should strike out on your own; become self-employed. Hardworking self-employed men and women in many fields are commonplace because they can earn more money when they set out on their own. Independent craftsmen and women can charge whatever the traffic will bear. Freelance typing, translating, computer repair as well as numerous kinds of alternative medical treatment are just a few of the career avenues Israelis follow. However, new immigrants, especially those raised in the former Soviet Union where independent economic activity was discouraged and often illegal, find it hard to choose these options. Immigrants from France, where standards are high and formal credentials are appreciated, face a difficult reality in Israel where repairmen and artisans sometimes cut corners and clients want to save money. But eventually they learn to compete with veteran Israeli craftsmen.

As is true elsewhere, unskilled or semi-skilled employment in construction, hotels, agriculture and care giving is low paying. As a rule Arabs work in hotels, Thais work in agriculture, Romanians and Chinese fill construction jobs and Filipinos take care of the elderly and some of the handicapped. The Interior Ministry has a special police unit that seeks out illegal foreign workers and initiates deportation proceedings. As a response to this policy, there are several voluntary organizations that assist foreign workers in their confrontation with the law and advise Israelis who wish to employ foreigners.

Starting in 1992, Israel's high tech sector took off exponentially and now accounts for about 25% of the GNP. There are miniature Silicon Valleys in Haifa, Jerusalem, Herzliya and Rehovot. Venture capital investors do well in Israel and many start-up companies are successful. On 20 July 2007 I turned to the financial pages of the *Jerusalem Post* and counted no less than 91 Israeli companies listed on the NASDAQ stock exchange. Other firms like Amdocs, a world leader in producing computer billing software that enables users to pay their bills by phone and chalks up an annual net profit of over 88 million dollars, are listed on the NYSE. Amdoc's stock keeps going up.

Immigrant scientists and technicians have made enormous contributions to the economy which keeps growing at four to five percent a year despite enemy activities. As an employment advisor I personally sent many newcomers to government-run training courses that updated their knowledge. This was necessary because East European standards and systems were inferior to or incompatible with the more advanced Western technologies extant in Israel. Technicians who complete these courses invariably increase their employability.

Briefly, Israel started out as a socialist economy in which the government played a dominant role. More recently, the economy has been liberalized through privatization. The shekel has been floated and is increasing in value with respect to the US dollar. Emphasis is on entrepreneurship. There are over 400,000 private companies in Israel. Every year many firms declare bankruptcy but they are replaced by even more start-ups. As in the U.S., people with technical qualifications find employment in science-based companies while others can earn a living in the service sector.

Finding a place to live presents a different sort of problem because virtually all flats are owned by and rented from private individuals. Commercial rental housing is essentially non-existent because Israel follows the U.K. system where every family expects to buy and wants to live in its own flat. Apartments are, for the most part, still owner-occupied and relatively expensive in comparison to Europe and America. Every flat is assessed a monthly maintenance fee which enables the residents' building committee to carry out repairs and pay for janitorial services.

Many singles, students and foreign workers seek out low-cost rentals in older neighborhoods. Today the situation is a bit more complex because many wealthy Americans and Europeans spend a few months or years in Netanya, Jerusalem and other attractive cities and then return home. These foreign temporary residents prefer larger, more modern rental accommodations. Fortunately for them, spacious apartments are available because some Israelis have been able to purchase second flats and a sizable number of individuals based overseas have also bought apartments as investments. A slump in the general real estate market a few years ago did not affect the construction and sale of luxury units. Today Israel is a small country with a high population density. Twenty and thirty story buildings are now commonplace in the Tel Aviv area.

During the last two decades there has been a significant increase in the number of private homes. People who can afford their own 'villa' usually have enough money to decorate and furnish it in a fashion that parallels similar dwellings abroad. IKEA is about to open a second home furnishing store because it is doing a brisk business in Israel. A modern life style includes automobiles, electronic gadgets, computers and, in some instances, swimming pools.

East European type mass housing estates are no longer being built. The Spartan studio apartments common to kibbutzim have pretty much been replaced with more comfortable quarters.

The cost of housing varies greatly and reflects location more than anything else. The further you are from city centers, the less you have to spend on housing. The government subsidizes housing for lower income people in several ways, including small grants and low-interest mortgages for young couples, but these programs are being cut back in line with the adoption of free-market principles. There are, consequently, people who cannot afford to buy their own apartments. Unfortunately, a few homeless men and women can be found in Israel as they are elsewhere.

Health insurance is compulsory in Israel. Everyone remits two National Insurance Institute taxes each month; one covers medical care provided by private sick fund clinics while the second assessment relates to everything else (i.e. workman's compensation, accident, unemployment and disability insurance as well as compensation to victims of Arab terror attacks). The four main sick funds have clinics all over the country. The system is similar to the one found in Germany where people belong to the clinics of their choice. However, treatment at spas which is funded in Germany is not covered in Israel. Each doctor enrolls large numbers of patients for whom she or he is responsible. The care received for routine illnesses and minor aches and pains from these general practitioners is adequate. However, whenever serious problems that warrant optimum attention arise, people prefer to go to an expert of their choice. This is called *sharap* which is an acronym for 'private medical service'. The difference is clear: when my son was ill we went to a specialist via *sharap* who spent an hour and a half with us explaining all the intricacies of his condition. This could never happen at a health fund clinic because of the pressures under which staff doctors work. Each doctor sees dozens of patients every day. Only ten or fifteen minutes are allotted for each visit but more time is often needed to render proper treatment. Sometimes, one of the doctor's patients who does not have an appointment appears unexpectedly because of an emergency that requires the doctor's immediate attention.

The British complain about their national medical care system and believe it is inferior to the French one. Similarly, sharp criticism has been voiced in Israel about expensive operations and costly drugs that are not paid for under the national insurance scheme. These complaints make for loud, scandalous headlines because it is taken for granted that Israel has to demonstrate greater humanitarian concern than one finds in other countries and the money to pay for it must be made available. By and large, Israel's system of independent sick fund clinics serves the public well.

It is axiomatic that husbands and wives both go out to work. Therefore, a comprehensive system of day care centers and kindergartens has been in place for a long time so that both parents are free to work. Many women work as nannies, but the vast majority of pre-school children attend well-equipped child care centers. Emunah, the religious women's organization, WIZO (Women's International Zionist Organization) and Naamat which operates under Histadrut auspices each run nationwide networks of pre-school facilities. There are also many privately run day care centers and some cities operate programs that allow mothers to care for up to five additional children in their homes. From age three to six when children enter first grade almost all have spent several years learning basic school skills and socializing with their peers in day care centers and kindergartens.

Education in Israel is characterized by diversity and disparities. Instead of one monolithic system such as that found in Japan where the Ministry of Education implements a single curriculum and teaching plan throughout the entire country, Israel has several largely autonomous school systems. First, there are regular public schools (grades 1-12) that serve the mainstream secular population. The Ministry of Education also operates schools for religiously observant communities. Pupils in this system are exposed to much more Bible and Judaic studies. After school hours, secular children can join the scouts (boys and girls meet together) or other secular youth movements while observant youngsters socialize within the B'nei Akiva framework for religious youth. Contact between secular and religious youth is generally minimal even when, as in my neighborhood, the two elementary schools are located less than a hundred meters apart and there are branches of the various youth movements functioning well.

A few exceptionally concerned citizen groups operate their own schools. In Jerusalem there is a 'traditional' school that brings both religious and secular children together in an attempt to bridge the gap between the two. There are also 'experimental' schools employing approaches that encourage the cultivation of individual learning skills. Since 1989 over one million new immigrants from the former Soviet Union and its satellite countries have immigrated to Israel. Consequently, some activist parents have created yet another small school system that caters to this population by putting greater emphasis on math and science as was the rule in the USSR.

The ultra-religious camp is divided into several independent sects; each running its own '*yeshivas*' where male and female students separately study the Torah and Talmud intensely with little time given over to math, science, English and other secular subjects. These *yeshiva* pupils learn little about Zionism and Israel's modern history. Within this sector of the populace we find a wide range of ideologies from the miniscule anti-Zionist Natorei Karta sect on the one hand and on the other hand, the large pro-Israel Chabad organization that has enthusiastic emissaries literally all over the world who bring Jewish ritual, spirituality and culture to far flung Jewish communities.

Arab children attend Arab language schools but it is quite rare to find an Arab boy or girl who has not mastered Hebrew. Large numbers of Arab students successfully pass the matriculation examinations and are accepted by colleges and universities in significant numbers. One educator at the Western Galilee College estimates that 40% of the college's student body is Arab. Many of these Arab students are activists. A few years ago they demanded that the College provide them with a mosque that would parallel the synagogue that serves the Jewish student body. Arab students are also active on behalf of Palestinian causes and frequently criticize government policies sharply.

Some Arab high schools in east Jerusalem follow the Jordanian syllabi and their students take the Jordanian matriculation exams. Very wealthy Arab and some Jewish families send their children to international schools run by the British and French in Jerusalem and the Americans in Kfar Shmaryahu, near Tel Aviv. There are also church-related (e.g. Lutheran, Catholic and Armenian) schools; the best known being St. George's Anglican school in east Jerusalem about two hundred meters down the road from the American Consulate General.

Many Jewish and Arab students go abroad to attend universities in the U.S., Hungary (where English language instruction is available), Italy (which has a sort of open-enrollment system that places the onus on a student's self-discipline) and elsewhere. Young men and women who cannot afford to study abroad can easily attend local branches of foreign universities, most of which are not recognized by Israel's Council of Higher Education. However, some courses of study taught at Touro College do have official approval.

Life in Israel is not easy. A Ministry of Immigrant Absorption poster declares that, "we never promised you a rose garden". Indeed, there are many government-sponsored programs and private organizations to assist newcomers. When I worked for the Employment Service I compiled a list of twenty-two bodies that also offered job placement, career counseling and vocational training to new *olim*. Everyone can find a place in Israel but it takes patience and fortitude. One learns how the various support systems function and, simultaneously, internalizes the values upon which interpersonal relations are based.

3
THE SABRA PERSONA

Every society is complex because human cultures are a composite of ever-changing beliefs, values, fears, superstitions, mores and much more. New conventions supplant or modify old customs to steer societies into unanticipated directions. Nevertheless, enduring behavioral standards often characterize people in different societies over long periods, lending stability to their lives. For instance, the Dutch are known for their extreme frugality, the Japanese emphasize politeness and refer to their society as a *'consideration culture'* while the French stress elegance and *savoir faire* or knowing how to act in a fresh, witty and original manner.

In Israel, more than anyplace else, nobody wants to be a *frier*. Every effort is made to avoid being a *frier* because *friers* are suckers, dupes and, most especially, fall-guys. No one wants to lose to a more sophisticated competitor.

To navigate well in a contentious social milieu one must be assertive and ready to fight for one's rights and agenda. Being frank and verbally aggressive is a tactic employed to advance one's position and protect oneself. No Israeli wants to become someone else's *frier*. Pushing to the front of a line, bargaining hard for a better price and taking shortcuts at work are techniques employed by Israelis to be successful and avoid the low status of a *frier*.

For example, when an Israeli gets into a taxi-cab he is likely to ask, 'How much does it cost to get to Herzl Boulevard?' The driver will respond with, 'Do you want to go by the meter or not?' The metered fare includes a 15% value added tax. By not using the meter, both driver and passenger avoid paying the VAT tax. Similarly, when you ask a plumber for a repair estimate he will probably enquire, 'Are you going to pay cash or by check and do you need a receipt?' People who hire painters and other repairmen frequently prefer to pay cash, skip the receipt and thereby save some money. Those who do not can be classified as *friers*.

Israeli motorists do everything legally and sometimes illegally on the roads to avoid being *friers*. I would guess that a majority of Israeli drivers hit the accelerator pedal the moment they see a traffic light switch from green to yellow. They know that they are supposed to brake for the imminent red light but why slow down (behave like a *frier*) when you have a chance of beating the red light.

Not surprisingly, one of the most common causes of fatal and non-fatal traffic accidents is cars running red lights. In fact, Israel has a high traffic death rate. Since the founding of the state in 1948, more people have been killed on the roads than in all the Arab wars and terror attacks. A large percentage of these victims have been children and the elderly.

To get approaching vehicles to slow down and stop so pedestrians at clearly marked and well lit crosswalks can safely cross the street, people have to step into the roadway, hope for the best and proceed at some risk. With the advent of drivers chatting away on mobile phones instead of concentrating on their driving, there has been an increase in the number of collisions. This is the situation despite a law that prohibits using cell phones in automobiles unless properly mounted. But I have never heard of a driver being charged with this offence.

To avoid being a *frier* that plays by the rules, drivers think little or nothing about going over the speed limit. When stuck in a traffic jam some wise guys will take advantage of the road's shoulder (reserved for emergency vehicle use only) to pass the *friers* crawling along in proper lanes. When street-smart drivers encounter a long line of cars creeping along in the right-turn or left-turn lane, they often drive around the *friers* and then nose their way back into the line when they get closer to the intersection. If the *friers* who stayed patiently in line want to keep the smart alecks from re-entering the line, they have to maintain a tiny distance of a few centimeters between their cars and the vehicles in front of them. In this connection, we should note that failure to maintain a safe distance between cars is another major cause of accidents on the roads.

After violating so many traffic rules and regulations, the average Israeli driver thinks little about parking in a restricted zone. I've witnessed arguments break out between parking wardens and irate drivers protesting freshly-written tickets. In fact, parking fines are now a major source of income for Israel's overcrowded cities. However, few Israelis are willing to forego private transportation even when they find themselves moving at a snail's pace through city streets where parking is a big problem and expense.

Israelis refuse to be *friers* on the highways or in any other sphere of life. For instance, I exercise at a well-equipped sports center several times a week whose dressing room is somewhat small for the number of men working out at the center. There are an ample number of lockers nearby in the corridor right next to the changing room but most of the sportsmen simply leave their pants and belongings in the dressing room in defiance of the manager's pleas to use the lockers and thus leave enough space for others who come later. Taking one's street clothes to the lockers, however, requires a bit of extra effort that only a *frier* like me is willing to make.

Every apartment building in my neighborhood has its own garbage bins that are normally located behind the buildings, out of sight. But many, perhaps most, residents do not go around back to dispose of their refuse in *their* bins. Instead they throw their trash into other, more convenient bins that they pass on their way to wherever they are going. As a consequence of this behavior, there are many over-flowing garbage cans in my area while others remain half empty because the majority of my neighbors are not *friers* who go out of their way to the back of the buildings to toss their garbage where it belongs.

The *frier* problem in Israel becomes serious when it interferes with reserve army duty. Theoretically, every citizen is supposed to serve three years in the army and then do annual reserve duty until about age 45. However, large numbers of young men and women find ways of avoiding enlistment or dodging reserve service obligations. The patriotic reservists who continue to show up for army duty and carry the burden of national defense increasingly feel that they are *friers* and resent those sectors of the population that do not share in the national defense effort.

Chutzpah (nerve and audacity) is a well-known Israeli character trait that helps one to avoid becoming a *frier*.

On May 14, 1948, when Ben-Gurion declared Israel's independence, some contemporaries thought that this proclamation was premature because seven Arab armies were invading the country and Field Marshall Montgomery predicted that the infant Jewish state was going to be wiped out within a few weeks. Declaring independence was, indeed, *chutzpah* on an epic level.

Chutzpah normally requires nerve and courage to do something quite unexpected. It can take the form of a positive proactive initiative or it may be a reaction to something or somebody else's actions.

In February 1968 Abie Nathan flew his own plane to Egypt as a private peace promotion effort. That was *chutzpah* in action! Many Mosad operations such as the capture of Adolf Eichmann in Argentina are examples of *chutzpah*. Rescuing hijacked plane hostages at Entebbe (1976) and a few years later flying thousands of Ethiopian Jews out of the Sudan, a bitter enemy state, are more examples of *chutzpah* in action.

When I first arrived in Israel in 1969 I often heard a common refrain, 'the difficult we do immediately but the impossible takes a little longer'. *Chutzpah*, a bit of arrogance and an overdose of self-esteem are basic ingredients in the national character. It is not surprising, therefore, that tourists can buy a t-shirt that declares, "Don't worry America, Israel is behind you".

Chutzpah can be found almost everywhere. For example, Israeli farmers export tulips to Holland where these flowers mature later.

Chutzpah can also be quite annoying at times. Taxi drivers who stop in the middle of the street to pick up or drop off passengers make me angry. But bus drivers who do the same thing are usually trying to be extra helpful to old folks even though they can be heavily fined for this infraction.

Israelis like to give the impression that they know everything. They do their best not to look stupid. I encountered this trait when I was a newcomer and had to ask directions often. When I asked passersby for directions, some would provide false information while others guided me to my destination. But I can't recall anyone simply saying, "I don't know".

Years later at my office I would occasionally confess to my colleagues that "I don't know" when I was unfamiliar with a particular subject. My co-workers invariably appeared surprised by this reply and couldn't make sense of this strange declaration. It was like asking for bread in a Chinese restaurant. Instead of admitting that they lack pertinent information to form an opinion, Israelis most often prefer to speak up even when their knowledge of a given topic is minimal.

Some Israelis also assume that there is little they need to learn. Israeli business people who fly off to exotic destinations to market their products devote less time to intercultural training than their American and European counterparts do. Israelis feel that their instincts are enough to facilitate success anywhere. Naturally, it is in the field of international travel that Israelis consider themselves especially perceptive. Most Israeli travelers believe they know where to get the cheapest accommodations and best bargains just about anywhere in the world.

Knowing a lot, of course, requires plenty of informal research; talking to as many people as possible and asking direct, pertinent questions. This also explains why there are no taboo questions in Israel. People regularly ask strangers how much they earn, how high their mortgage is and how much did they pay for their car, etc. Lack of inhibition and informality infuse social interaction. Everyone is on a first name basis with everyone else. When you hear a speaker use someone's **last** name or a **title**, he or she is probably critical of that person or wants to distance himself from the man or woman in question.

Another Israeli trait that stands out is the predisposition to humanitarianism. Israel as a nation and Israelis as individuals are quick to respond whenever natural or man-made catastrophes occur; lending a helping hand by whatever means called for. When an earthquake leveled a sizable city in Turkey a few years ago the government sent its special army emergency rescue unit to help. When the Christmas 2004 tsunami hit Thailand and the Indian Ocean area a public appeal was immediately launched to raise funds for search and rescue missions. Blacks escaping from the Sudan in 2007 and crossing illegally into Israel have been accommodated at hotels. Others who were arrested quickly came to the attention of human rights activists who pressured the government to release most of them.

Israeli doctors can be found in remote villages in Africa and Vietnam doing their best to improve health standards in these distant places.

Similarly, volunteer groups in Israel assist illegal migrant workers from West Africa. Left-wing activists, ignoring Palestinian aggression, provide legal aid to Palestinians, promote Palestinian human rights, help harvest their olive crop and sympathize with the Palestinian cause and thereby undermine Israel's political position. In addition, there are many groups promoting animal rights, medical research and many more humanitarian causes. Voluntarism is widespread in many spheres. Both secular and religious individuals help out formally within institutional frameworks or informally on their own. Every day I see people feeding the alley cats that are carefully watched by jealous crows. Other volunteers collect old clothes and appliances for the needy.

Israelis support a large number of charities such as *Yad Sarah* which is an organization with branches all over the country. *Yad Sarah* lends free medical equipment to people in need of wheel chairs, crutches and other paraphernalia. Sister organizations offer ambulance and transportation services to handicapped people. In the ultra religious sector of the population there are *gemach* groups that provide free loans, wedding dresses and other items to impoverished recipients.

Israelis are definitely a compassionate people. Some would say that this is a way of expressing the idea that 'Jews are God's chosen people' while others remind us that Jews have a two thousand year history of being oppressed so it is only natural for Israelis to identify with and rush to help strangers in trouble. Even "moderate" Fatah terrorists escaping from Hamas terrorists after their brief civil war in Gaza in 2007 were protected. Doing nothing is rarely an option in Israeli thinking. One must react, take charge, and espouse a *big head* (i.e. display initiative).

As a nation under constant threat, Israel has, as a matter of self-preservation, created a first-rate citizen army. Basic training for eighteen year old recruits is intensive and can last for as long as six months. Soldiers, both men and women, are taught to work as a team but also to take initiatives. Officers are expected to always be in front of their troops, leading the charge forward. This dynamism carries over into civilian life in many ways. Israel has a high percentage of entrepreneurs. High tech "incubators" often succeed in creating new companies and original products no one ever thought of before. Kibbutzim (cooperative villages) are by definition dynamic because economic activities and social policies are constantly examined and, if need be, revised. The kibbutzim are famous for their ethos of hard work and enterprise. Israel also has one of the highest rates of patent registration in the world. The pace of life on city streets equals New York City's frenzy.

Visitors readily feel Israel's abundant nervous energy wherever they go. People pushing their way onto buses whose drivers sometimes handle their vehicles as if they were race cars. Football all-stars radiate as much spunk as Brazil's national team but tend to score fewer goals. Youngsters pile into ancient amphitheaters to jump to the beat of Israeli rock music. Hiking in Israel as well as trekking in the Andes or Nepal attract disproportionate numbers of Israeli youth after they complete their army service.

Finns have been described as quiet people who limit themselves verbally. It is said that they keep too much of their inner tensions to themselves and thereby endanger their own mental and physical health. The very opposite is true of Israelis. Exceedingly sociable, Israelis easily strike up conversations with strangers; compatriots and foreigners alike. In contrast to the Japanese and other notably ethnocentric peoples, Israelis evince little or no anti-foreign sentiments. Not even Arabs are denigrated. I would say that those on the right side of the political debate arena are apprehensive and fearful of Arabs while leftists are generally supportive of Arab positions and sympathetic to their demands.

When debating controversies amongst themselves, garrulous Israelis easily drift into verbal aggression. When refuting others, ordinary Israelis use many phrases that call into doubt their respondent's intelligence and supposed normal mental state. I have compiled a short list of popular expressions Israelis employ when demolishing an opponent's arguments. Here are a few examples: *chachmologue* is derived from the word for *wisdom* and is equivalent to *wise guy*; *psychi*, pronounced *pseechee* roughly equates with *nut* (insane) in English; *maniac* refers to an unstable *nut* that is capable of doing anything; a *tembel* is naïve or just stupid and *mifager* is a retarded individual.

Israelis whose families emigrated from Kurdistan have been perversely stereotyped as stupid. Within the heat of hot debates this prejudice is sometimes expressed rhetorically by the query: "Are you a Kurd?" This is a direct assault on an adversary's intellectual abilities even if his forebears originated in Morocco or Poland.

Israeli speech is full of allusions to intelligence and aberrant mental states. *Not normal, stupid, crazy, not logical, use common sense, have you left your senses,* and *the Jewish head* (referring to mythical superior brain power) are just a few of the common expressions that pepper verbal intercourse. I suspect that this linguistic belligerence has a lot to do with the atmosphere of uncertainty that pervades the country. Having lived in the peaceful and polite rural Philippines many years ago, I can compare assertive Israeli verbal thrusts to the single disparaging word I learned there. *Gago* which means silly was taken as good-natured criticism and not as an insult by the Filipinos I met.

Although Israelis are hyperactive they also have, paradoxically, a fatalistic streak. The common idioms, *y'yeh b'seder* and *'y'yeh tov* (It will be alright, It's going to turn out well) are really statements that admit (1) there is a problem, (2) there is not much we can do about it and (3) let's hope for the best. Fatalism also allows both religious and secular sectors of the populace to find common ground. After all, they are sharing the very same reality and destiny despite the significant differences that divide them. Individuals in both groups frequently add *b'ezrat hashem* (with God's help) to their commentaries.

It is a truism that Israelis are constantly talking or, more accurately, arguing about politics. Once, a member of the MFO, Multinational Force and Observers (the eleven member international contingent stationed in Sinai that monitors Egyptian and Israeli compliance with the military limitations that the Israeli-Egyptian peace treaty places on both countries) showed me the manual each MFO observer gets when assigned to Sinai. On the very first page of the section outlining Israeli cultural attributes one learns that Israelis are always talking about politics. Whereas in Britain people like to chat about the weather and in the Philippines food is of much interest, Israelis skip the trivia and discuss politics at length.

Neighbors and friends constantly debate political issues because there is always something new to relate to. They enjoy a steady supply of new topics because hardly a day goes by in which some political figure is not publicly criticized or investigated. And most Israelis are only two or three rungs away from an influential person. We, therefore, have to take a closer look at Israeli politics.

4
POLITICS IN THE AIR EVERYWHERE

On Friday mornings, before the Sabbath, men often visit their favorite neighborhood café where they meet old friends to discuss current affairs. These informal debating groups coalesce into 'parliaments' that review and analyze the country's latest problems and suggest solutions. A lot of supposed 'inside', confidential information gets bandied about because it is difficult to keep secrets in Israel.

The Friday ad hoc commentators firmly believe that they live in a democracy because they are free to speak their minds. After all, doesn't free speech equate with and even define democracy? Moreover, politicians and media pundits constantly project themselves as defenders of Israeli democracy. Often, when a Knesset member is against a proposed law, he or she will warn the public that the new legislation endangers Israel's democratic society. But no one, as far as I know, has taken the trouble to distinguish between free speech as a civil liberty and democracy as a system of government.

Unfortunately, Israel is not a democracy. I repeat it is not a democracy. Israel is a *partyocracy*, what the Italians call a *partitocrazia*. While it is true that Israelis get to vote to fill 120 Knesset seats at least once in four years, it is also true that there are practically no democratic institutions as found in Western countries.

For starters, Israel does not have a constitution although there are some general basic laws that can be interpreted any way the courts like. Many people recognize the need for a constitution but no constitutional convention has ever been organized and no strong political force is pursuing this matter because it is an issue that generates serious disagreement. Ultra religious spokesmen proclaim that the Torah is their constitution.

The Supreme Court acts as a court of final appeals and simultaneously as a constitutional court. The Supreme Court has voided many Knesset laws declaring them invalid even though there is no constitution. In 2006 when Knesset committees examined the idea of creating a constitutional court and thereby relieve the Supreme Court of this function, Aharon Barak, the ultra-activist Chief Justice descended on the Knesset and effectively lobbied to abort this proposal at its conception. Barak would not consider any diminution of the powers he had relegated to himself. Many jurists in Israel and abroad believe that the classic tripartite balance of power is weighted in favor of the judiciary.

With just one insignificant exception, all of the Supreme Court's decisions have coincided with Chief Justice Barak's opinions. The Chief Justice of Israel is a powerful personage who is not subject to confirmation by the citizenry or by a vote in the Knesset. He, like all the members of the Supreme Court, is chosen by a nine member committee in which three are already Supreme Court justices. Essentially, no one gets to be a judge in Israel unless the justices sitting on the selection committee are satisfied with the candidate's politically correct credentials. No nationalistic, ultra-orthodox or independent thinking jurist has a chance of getting a place on the bench. For example, Professor Ruth Gavison, a well-known and highly respected academic was an excellent candidate for the high court but was rejected by Barak because, as he put it, "she has an agenda". Since Gavison's legal opinions do not coincide with Barak's exceedingly liberal values as demonstrated by his belief that every possible issue is within the purview of the court, the selection committee chaired by Barak before his retirement rejected her candidacy and no one could do anything about it.

Many advocacy groups have organized mass demonstrations and petitions signed by hundreds of thousands of concerned citizens but there is no mechanism for translating the public's wishes into action. Israel has no system of referendums, plebiscites, and citizen initiatives or recall of elected officials. The Knesset can expel a particularly errant or criminal lawmaker and impeach the President but this has never happened. The interior minister can suspend a local council mayor but this is a rare occurrence. The Knesset ethics committee does review misconduct but follow-up penalties are almost unheard of because of political in-fighting that usually results in stalemates.

The political system is based on general elections that are held every four years or whenever a government falls. Eligible voters from eighteen years of age get the chance to cast one single ballot for their favorite **party**. That's it! Israelis do not elect candidates; they choose party lists. Invariably, a party's list contains the names of people you like or dislike or just don't know. As most parties don't have a primary system, the people on a party's list are chosen by an in-group or central committee or by an all-powerful party chairman. The larger parties, Likud and Labor do hold primaries but, unlike primaries in the US which are open to anyone who wishes to register either as a Republican or Democrat, these are open only to dues paying party members. Media coverage of both Likud and Labor primaries has often included reports of bribery and other underhanded deals made by unscrupulous contenders who, naturally enough, do their best to project an image of honesty and patriotism.

A party has to get at least 2% of the popular vote in order to secure a seat in the Knesset. A few years ago Penina Rosenblum, a well-known celebrity and founder of her own successful cosmetics company failed to attain the threshold by just a few thousand votes. The same was true of the pensioners' party until the 2006 election in which they surprisingly attained seven Knesset seats and joined Olmert's coalition government. One explanation given for their unexpected success suggests that many voters, especially young people, are so disillusioned with the mainstream parties that they cast their ballots for *Gil*, the pensioners' party as a protest against the establishment.

Attempts to raise the threshold percentage to 5% as it is in Germany have failed. Consequently, no fewer than twelve parties get elected to every Knesset. The system is characterized, as in Italy, by instability because coalition governments are composed of parties many of whom compete with or are antagonistic to one another. For example, the Olmert government is made up of Kadima and Labor who are rivals. It also included Yisrael Beteinu, a right-wing party that opposes Labor's political program and vice versa. These two coalition partners despised each other but the love of power bound them to the coalition until Yisrael Beteinu quit the government.

Not popularly elected, Knesset members are beholden to the activists who worked hard on their behalf to get them placed high enough on their party's list so as to attain their places in parliament. Former Prime Minister Ariel Sharon's son Omri was convicted of violating political party financing regulations while Naomi Blumenthal was convicted of bribing (i.e. paying for hotel accommodations) Likud central committee members to vote her onto the Likud list thereby getting herself re-elected to the Knesset. Blumenthal was subsequently sentenced to 6 months community service. The Knesset ethics committee also scrutinized Shimon Peres' receipt of a $100,000. "gift" during his failed campaign to get elected to lead the Labor party. Ultimately, Peres left Labor to join Kadima and subsequently got himself elected president by successfully appealing to the religious parties including Shas (Sephardim). As a staunch socialist, Peres has nothing in common with any of these biblical traditionalists. Political expediency makes for strange bedfellows.

As Knesset members do not have constituencies and since there are no electoral districts to represent, politicians easily change their policy positions, alter their ideologies and switch parties (which is quite common) in accordance with their personal strategies of getting elected so as to enjoy the prestige, perks and power of office.

Many Israelis and Israeli institutions are identified with a political movement or party. For example, the General Kupat Holim (the largest chain of health clinics) was once an integral part of the Histadrut labor unions organization which in turn was an informal arm of the Labor party. Likewise, the smaller National Kupat Holim is aligned with the Likud party's institutions. The various religious parties operate their own school systems whose curriculums differ significantly from the Ministry of Education's syllabi.

The Kibbutz (cooperative villages) and Moshav (family-based villages) Movement is aligned with the Labor party but the smaller religious kibbutz movement identifies with the national religious camp. Similarly, the B'nei Akiva youth movement is sponsored by the national religious Zionists while the Noar Oved V'Lomed (Youth Working and Studying) program is run by the Histadrut, General Federation of Labor. To its right, the Betar youth organization is part of the Likud's political constellation and endeavors to carry on Ze'ev Jabotinsky's and Menachem Begin's national Zionist vision.

Israel's political parties are really **lobbies** representing divergent sectors of the populace that differ substantively and are frequently in conflict with one another. I have heard people opine that if there were no Arab/Islamic existential threat to the country, these parties would probably be at each other's throats. What actually happens is that parties and their leaders rise, fall and disappear from the political venue. The larger parties survive but change their character and composition over time.

Israel's Labor party is the party of choice for retired IDF generals. The party's leadership today features many men whose first career was in the armed forces. Only four of eighteen former chiefs of staff have <u>not</u> gone into politics. The ex-generals pay lip service to social-democratic principles but they are all graduates of a distinctly undemocratic military milieu. Yitzhak Rabin and Ehud Barak are typical examples of men who rose through the ranks to become chief of staff, then on to minister of defense and finally prime minister. Israel is a little like Thailand in that one general takes over from another but without the seventeen or eighteen coups over some sixty years that have marked political change in Bangkok.

The Likud likes to project itself as the leader of the national camp but within the party we find numerous cliques of followers who support competing individuals who pragmatically modify their views leftward in line with the prevailing political winds. Intra-party discord seems to be characteristic of all parties and sometimes leads to a split out of which new splinter parties are born. When a particular leader is appointed to head a government ministry or serve as a director-general, he or she immediately distributes jobs to followers in his entourage. Tsahi Hanegbi, currently chairman of the Knesset's security and foreign affairs committee, is facing possible prosecution for appointing sixty-nine of his supporters when he took over the Ministry of Environmental Protection when the Likud came to power under Sharon. (Hanegbi is now in Kadima).

At a Likud party convention a few years ago Limor Livnat, a party stalwart and former Minister of Education, was at the podium preaching about national imperatives and asked rhetorically, "Are we Likudniks here only for the jobs?" and with unabashed spontaneity her audience shouted back "yes", "yes" to her great embarrassment.

The Shas party has in the past gotten as many as seventeen Knesset seats because its supporters, traditional religious Sephardim, constitute a very large segment of the population and have absolute faith in Rabbi Ovadia Yoseph, the party's spiritual as well as de facto leader who is assisted by a council of Torah sages. Shas has joined several coalition governments and, so long as its large school system receives sizable budgetary allotments, will vote with the government even if it is in disagreement in principle. Every party, most especially the smaller ones, represents a tight-knit socio-cultural community that shares specific values and political objectives. Despite disclaimers, party leaders take a keen interest in government jobs and seek subsidies to party-sponsored institutions. For example, a news item in *Haaretz* on June 15, 2007 reports that the Degel HaTorah (Torah Flag) party that represents some of the ultra-orthodox Ashkenazim apparently instructed its Knesset members to vote for Shimon Peres for president because he (Peres) had intimated that he would endeavor to have the gay pride parade in Jerusalem cancelled.

Shinui was a party whose platform was based on promoting secularism and opposition to the religious establishment. Shinui advocated civil marriage (which does not yet exist in Israel), reform conversions (that are not recognized by the Rabbinate), shopping on Saturday (which is repugnant to observant Jews) and the general principle of 'the separation of church and state'. Shinui, after internal squabbling, fell apart and failed to win any seats in the 2006 election but its anti-religious initiatives are endorsed by secular Israelis.

Supporters of the national religious Zionist camp are easily recognized by their colorful knitted skull caps. This element is arguably Israel's most idealistic sector that exerted enormous energy to prevent the expulsion of Jews from Gush Katif, Gaza and northern Samaria in August of 2005. The modern, orthodox Jewish, nationalistic lifestyle embodies Israel's positive pioneering values of hard work, volunteerism and dedication to the country. Men wearing knitted skull caps have increasingly replaced kibbutzniks in the army and now comprise about 50% of the officer corps. This community is represented by the NRP, National Religious Party and the National Union party but fail to return more that nine or ten members to the Knesset at election time.

Although Israel is now accused of being an apartheid state by Jimmy Carter and others, over twenty percent of the population is Arab. Arabs are free to go about and live wherever they wish. Arab voters support various Arab political parties that have nine Knesset members. This is in addition to the Arab MKs who serve as representatives of left-wing parties such as Labor and Meretz. Galeb Majadle, an Arab member of the Labor party was appointed to the post of Minister of Science, Culture and Sport. He promotes Arab interests in general and identifies with his brethren in Syria and other Arab lands. He was also responsible for the creation of an Arabic Language Academy to parallel the Hebrew Language Academy in Jerusalem even though there are twenty-two Arab countries and not one other Hebrew-speaking nation. Additionally, Egypt, Syria and five other Arab states already have academies.

There are several Arab parties in Israel. Chadash is a communist party that identified with the former Soviet Union and demands recognition of Arabs as a national minority in Israel. The Ram party advocates Islamic values and is oriented toward the Moslem Brotherhood, the very same loose organization that is repressed in Egypt and Syria and inspires Hamas which categorically denies Israel's right to exist. Taal is a small party headed by Dr. Ahmed Tibi who was an advisor to Yasser Arafat and supports Fatah. Tibi is a frequent guest on Israeli TV. I once heard him identify himself as a "Palestinian Arab living in southern Syria and possessing Israeli citizenship". The Balad party has four Knesset seats. Its head, Azmi Bishara is now on the run; he fled Israel before the slow-moving state prosecutor could indict him for treason after he had made several trips to Syria and Lebanon where he publicly met with Hizbullah leaders and emphatically urged them to continue with their war against the very country that paid (and apparently still pays) his salary and subsidizes his party.

A powerful force in Arab-Israeli politics is the Islamic movement's Northern Branch headed by Sheikh Ra'id Salah that disengaged itself from Ram when Ram decided to go into the Knesset and thereby confirm Israel's legitimacy. When assessing all these powerful anti-Israel forces extant in the Arab sector, it is hard to dismiss observers who see Israel's Arabs as a potential fifth column; something more to worry about. Moshe Feiglin, who was a contender for leadership in the Likud, writing in *Makor Rishon* (13 July 2007) cited an increasing number of Arab attacks on Jews in Israel proper. Arab demonstrators in Shefar'am carrying Palestinian flags burned the Israeli flag, clearly identify with their Palestinian kin. Recently, there was a report about an Israeli-Arab "liberation" group calling itself Ahrar al-Jalil (Free People of the Galilee).

I would guess that the overwhelming majority of Israelis do not see or wish to see any fifth column dangers. On the contrary, most media commentators take the position that the government doesn't do enough to advance Arab concerns. These people are inclined to support Meretz, the extreme left-wing party whose leader, Dr. Yossi Beilin along with Shimon Peres brought Arafat to Israel, helped him set up the Palestinian Authority in autonomous zones that quickly became convenient bases for increased terror attacks on Israel. At that time, Rabin and all those who enthusiastically supported the Oslo appeasement accords claimed that Arafat and his Fatah guerillas would control and subdue the more radical Hamas movement. Actually Arafat gave Hamas a franchise to dramatically increase its terror attacks on Israeli buses, markets and restaurants. Now that Hamas has a clear majority in the PA legislature and controls the Gaza strip, Meretz spokespersons like Zahava Gal-On are calling for an international force to quiet things down in Gaza and protect Israeli towns and villages in the area from Kassam rocket bombardments. Meretz generally accepts Arab complaints, vehemently objects to any Jewish presence in Judea and Samaria, ignores Jewish rights to these historic "occupied" territories and adheres to a revisionist history that primarily blames Israel for the never-ending Arab-Israel war. Meretz advocates even more concessions to Arab demands in the perennial search for peace. Meretz along with militant Arab parties and a large part of Israel's intelligentsia keeps pushing the nation leftward to oblivion. Some of the avant-garde radical leftists such as Avrum Burg, a former Labor party MK, ex-speaker of the Knesset, a former chairman of the Jewish Agency as well as the World Zionist Organization, believe that Israel was a mistake and has little right to exist. Burg's book, _Defeating Hitler_ suggests that Jews are paranoid and that Israel itself resembles Nazi Germany. It is astounding that many people who vote for Meretz and Labor can understand Burg's thesis which is founded on denying Israeli rights, ignoring Arab aggression, promoting false analogies to South Africa and a lot of self-hate.

To add insult to injury, left-wingers claim that Israeli settlement activities over the "green line" have caused an increase in corruption. But no examples of this supposed linkage have ever been presented. On the contrary, the Left's "peace process" does indeed have a direct link to corruption. The secret Oslo negotiations were in violation of the law that prohibits contact with enemy terror organizations. Political bribes were paid to people like former right-wing MK Alex Goldfarb (He got a good job and a Mitsubishi auto.) to vote for the Oslo agreement. Later, ex-Shin Bet assistant director Yossi Ginosar represented Israel in negotiations with Arafat and at the same time helped move Arafat's profits from the Jericho casino to banks in Switzerland. [Elyakim Rubinstein who was the attorney-general at the time looked into Ginosar's contradictory but financially rewarding activities. The case was closed and

Rubinstein was promoted to the Supreme Court.] Sharon's lawyer and advisor, Dov Weissglass represented Austrian billionaire Martin Schlaff who operated the Jericho casino for Arafat. The link between these three men and South African Cyril Kern has not yet been fully investigated (by Austrian and Israeli authorities) and explained to the public.

To recapitulate, the Israeli political system is a *partyocracy*. Each party represents a particular sector of the populace; secular, religious, ultra-religious, Arabs, leftists, rightists and even pensioners. Each party is essentially a *lobby* promoting its own narrow interests often at the expense of national goals. As Major-General (Res.) Giora Eiland, in a lecture I heard him deliver in April 2007, explains: it is very difficult for an Israeli government to function because so many different people and their parties are pulling in opposite directions. Eiland who served as the National Security Council's director found that the Prime Minister and the executive branch could not make objective decisions and take effective action even in crucial defense matters (e.g. the war in Lebanon in 2006) because coalition partners (i.e. self-centered parties with their own agendas) can pull the rug out from under at a moment's notice. It is always safer to do little or nothing so as not to disturb the status quo.

Nevertheless, the government has occasionally gone in the opposite direction, acting impulsively and dangerously. For example, Sharon and his Likud came to power on a platform that opposed the removal of Jewish settlements in Gaza's Gush Katif area and in northern Samaria. Sharon did an about-face, decided to forcibly expel the national-religious settlers from their homes. To this end he replaced the army's commander, Moshe Ya'alon and police chief with men more amenable to his plan. Under pressure from his own party to hold a national referendum, Sharon called for a Likud party referendum instead; which he **lost**. But, as this vote was unofficial and non-binding, he simply ignored its results and bullied most of his party's MKs and ministers into voting for his "disengagement" plan in the Knesset. This was the same plan he himself opposed when it was initially proposed by his Labor party opponent Amram Mitzna in the previous election campaign in 2003. A handful of party members remained faithful to the Likud's platform and nationalistic ethos. These loyalists voted against Sharon's Jewish expulsion project and were quickly branded "rebels" in the media which had abandoned all pretensions of objectivity or neutrality on this issue.

The Knesset has one hundred and twenty members. These men and women represent their parties and **not** the citizenry at large. Every seven years these party hacks elect a president who is the official head of state. Most of Israel's nine presidents have been politicians and not eminent academics or outstanding public figures. If Israel were a true democracy, the election of its president would be open to all its citizens. Candidates would have to explain publicly why they want to receive ambassadors, grant pardons and work hard to unify such a diverse, independent-minded and unruly population.

The Israeli *partyocracy* is highly dysfunctional when viewed as a system of government in its entirety. However, people who rely on their connections to party activists who help them solve personal problems are not interested in seeing changes made in the system. Even Ben-Gurion failed to change the system and diminish party power. Because most Israelis are so close to influential people, they think that they are participating in a true democracy. Citizens who make good use of their connections are invariably patriotic as well. Usually, but not always, there is no conflict between their self-interest and national concerns. Against this background, anti-corruption crusaders and political reform movements find it hard to make progress.

The *partyocracy* also maintains an unholy relationship with the agenda-driven media. Politically correct thinking is created by the intelligentsia and disseminated by writers, editors and commentators who adhere to axiomatic "truths". However, before scrutinizing the media's role in creating an imaginary reality based on false premises and a lot of wishful thinking, we will take a brief look at the Hebrew language as spoken today because it provides additional insights into the Israeli psyche.

5
ISRAELESE

The way a particular group of people expresses itself in its own tongue is a fairly accurate reflection of its unique orientation to life. The vernacular reflects the culture of which it is a part. This link between language and culture is definitely significant in Israel. The Israeli mentality expresses itself in the Hebrew language as it is actually spoken today on the streets of Tel Aviv and elsewhere in the country.

Hebrew, the language of the Bible, was considered a dead language until about a hundred years ago when it was revived for everyday use by Zionists. Once resuscitated, it took on a life of its own. Like English, Modern Hebrew seems to possess an almost infinite capacity to absorb words and idiomatic expressions from other languages. The number of foreign words in Hebrew today is enormous by any standard. Indeed, the Israeli mother tongue should be called *Israelese*.

Linguists are likely to place *Israelese* alongside of patois and Pidgin English. *Israelese* reminds me of Chepacano in the Philippines which is an amalgam of Spanish and a local dialect. Yiddish which is based on old German but contains a large number of Hebrew words and an assortment of terms from East European languages is also a compound idiom. In multi-ethnic Singapore a lingua franca called *Singlish* (a blend of Malay, Tamil and Chinese words added to English based on Chinese grammar) has emerged. *Israelese*, therefore, is not a unique phenomenon.

[Italicized words that follow are now part of the Hebrew language spoken today.]

A favorite coffee house chain in Jerusalem is called *Aroma*. Of course, you can buy *kafei* in a *supermarket* where you can also purchase *shampoo, cottage* (cheese), *soda, Coke, spaghetti, macaroni* and *biscuitim*. There may also be a choice of *bagels* and *sandwiches* (pronounced: sandvitchim).

Israelis also routinely eat *schnitzel, beefsteaks, hamburgers, pizzas* and *salatim*.

Famous corporations have branches in Israel. *Intel, Motorola, Digital, Dun and Bradstreet, McDonald's* and most of its competitors are household names in Israel. Furthermore, Israeli firms tend to adopt easily recognizable Latin-based names. *Sigma* (chemicals), *Elbit* (computers), *Israel Discount Bank, Multi-lock, Electra* (appliances) and *Alliance* (tires) are examples of Israeli companies active in the global marketplace.

When we turn our attention to small businesses and stores we find ourselves in a forest of foreign appellations with names such as *Printiv* (printers), *Panorama* (hotel), *El Gaucho* (restaurant), *Royalty* (jewelry), *Computmat* (computer sales), *Bug* (computer accessories), *Prisma* (photo shop) and *Hot* (heating systems). The list is practically endless.

Parents sometimes give their children international names. So you frequently meet Israelis called *Edna, Mickey, Suzy, Sandy, Molly, Vickie, Judy, Betty and Alice*. Names taken from the Bible include *Dan, Daniel, Dina and Sarah* are, of course, familiar to speakers of most European languages.

Television and radio commentators and the celebrities they interview literally bombard the public with terminology that features: *politica, democratia, platforma, legetimi* (legitimate), *pessimi* (pessimistic), *optimi, positivi, conceptsia, ritual, interesim, indicatorim, ratsional, temperatura,* and the all-important *proteksia* which refers to the power brokers a person can count on to get him what he desires before someone else beats him to it.

When Israelis, especially youngsters, bump into one another in the street their conversation normally starts with *'hi'* and ends with *'bye'* or *'see ya'*. When the kids approve of something or someone they will use *fantasti* (fantastic) or the slang *sababa* or its American equivalent, *'cool'*.

Israelis invariably start telephone conversations with *hallo*. A speaker is likely to introduce a topic by saying he wants to discuss, *le-daskess* a matter of mutual interest.

In the realm of sports, Israelis talk about the *liga* (league), *fou-lim* (fouls), and *offsides*. Sportscasters who covered the European light *athletica* competitions a few years ago in Berlin speculated about *favoritim* destined to come in first.

Muzika pop (pop music) is as Israeli as falafel balls. Singers bring out new *albomim* (albums) and *diskim* all the time hoping for a *hit* or *schlaga*. Once a year the local cinema industry awards *Israeli Oscars* (the Ophir Prizes). Sometimes the award goes to an old-timer who has made a *comeback*.

However, no one can surpass the *politikaim* (politicians) who excel in *Israelese*. Their polemics include *primaries, terroristim, sini* (cynical), *filabusta, dinamica, apozitsia* (the opposition), *competitzia, assertiviut* (assertiveness), *informatsia, disinformatsia, candidatim, constitusia, republica bananot* and *Israelbluff*.

Media pundits have a propensity to label almost every news event *histori* (historical). As native speakers of *Israelese*, they have fully integrated international terminology into their lexicons. *Automobilim, autobusim, telephonim, televisia, radio, boss, taxi, universita, muzeum, opera, comedia, ballet, farsa* (farce), *concert, veterinar* (veterinary doctor), *test, magazinim and cosmetica* are terms commonly used.

Flat tires are repaired by a *pankchermacher*. The universities are populated with *professors, doctors* and *studentim*.

Reuben Alcalay, who passed away in 1967, compiled a dictionary of foreign words and phrases in Hebrew. There is even a special term, *luazi* for these foreign words. This dictionary fills 398 pages.

The Hebrew Language Academy is located on the Hebrew University's Givat Ram campus in Jerusalem but its influence is negligible because most of the neologisms it invents are just not adopted into everyday speech by the public at large. The great disparity between the spoken idiom and standard or correct Hebrew as promoted by the Academy inspired several very successful comedy routines by Israel's premier entertainment trio, *Hagashash Hachiver* ("The Pale Tracker").

Foreign vocabulary and phrases such as *"take it easy"* and *"no problem"* are central elements in *Israelese*. This unconscious drive to turn Hebrew into a kind of Jewish Esperanto seems to indicate a deep need to be part of the wider world and be accepted by other nations. In addition, internationalizing the Hebrew language is one way of escaping the provincialism induced by living in a tiny country constantly exposed to external political pressures while still maintaining linguistic uniqueness.

Since so many Israelis were born abroad, it seems quite natural to employ phrases which are verbatim translations from other idioms. For instance, Israelis use *Comment appelez-vous?* (How are you called?) instead of the more proper *what's your name?*

Israelese is a fusion of foreign nouns and phrases and quite a few English verbs. It would be nice if everyone spoke a flowery biblical-like Hebrew but this is not the case. What we have is a lively language that serves the public as well as other languages serve their speakers. Additionally, *Israelese* speakers communicate well when overseas. Also, new immigrants seem to find it easy to learn this vernacular because it has so many transnational (especially English) components.

With basic fluency, Hebrew/*Israelese* speakers are ready to listen to radio and TV commentators. Making sense out of media reports, however, requires an additional set of faculties. To truly understand public speakers in Israel one has to know what a word or phrase really means in its original language and how these terms are being distorted by public orators. The next chapter explains why one must always question newscasters and commentators.

6
MEDIA POWER

Over sixty years ago George Orwell spotlighted the problem of group-think; how totalitarian regimes control and manipulate the news so that the general public correctly learns what's right and what's wrong. As a boy I remember my dad reading _Brain Washing in Red China_ during the 1950s. A joke that found its way out of the former Soviet Union declared that 'there is no pravda (truth) in _Isvestia_ (spark) and no isvestia in _Pravda'_. Today the Qatar-based Al-Jazeera satellite TV station can say almost anything it wants about Arab rulers except, of course, those who run the Qatari government. Al-Jazeera has irritated some Arab leaders such as Hosni Mubarak to the point that its reporters have been expelled from Egypt and other offended countries. Ironically, Al-Jazeera's reporter in Israel enjoys more freedom than his co-workers in many Arab lands despite his rabidly anti-Israel disposition. Indeed, insulting a public official in Egypt and elsewhere in the Arab world is a crime punishable by imprisonment.

Many years ago I read _Inventing Reality: The Politics of the Mass Media_ (1986) by Michael Parenti, a Harvard professor. Parenti claims that the US media is controlled by conservative, capitalistic forces and that liberal initiatives and social causes get little or no coverage. Furthermore, Parenti thinks that the US media is generally negative with regard to welfare programs and leftist interpretations of current affairs. By contrast, the Israeli media is leftist-dominated and casts right-wing nationalists in a negative light. This view of the Israeli media is corroborated by Amos Goren who served as the Israel Broadcasting Authority's ombudsman for six years until June 2007. In a farewell interview in *Makor Rishon* (22 June 2007) Goren summarizes his experiences and says:

> *"public media outlets that draw such a high percentage of complaints from one direction [the Right] must evaluate their performance very seriously. This is why my report advises that all sectors of the population should have proportional representation in the composition of the Broadcasting Authority's staff [which is overwhelmingly secular, liberal and leftist]".* Goren goes on to recall that *"there is an anti-Jerusalem and anti-settler spirit. A good word about Gush Katif [the Jewish settlements in Gaza] has almost never been broadcast; not even from a strictly agricultural perspective. [The Gush Katif settlements were agricultural successes that produced large quantities of cherry tomatoes for export and marketed sizable quantities of bug-free lettuce and other vegetables.] This is amazing and painful".* (Author's translation)

I clearly remember listening to the 10:00 a.m. news one rainy day in February 1988. This bulletin included a report about a bomb that had exploded in a trash basket in B'nei Brak near Tel Aviv. After the news, the Voice of Israel commentator hosting the *Hakal Diburim* program got an eye witness to the explosion on the phone and asked her what happened. The lady answered that a bomb had exploded "but thank goodness no one was hurt". Instantly, the radio mc asked, "And what about the two Arabs?" One Arab was injured and the other had been killed by his own bomb according to the news report. This sort of "balance" is standard in the Israeli media.

For years Shelly Yichimovitz was a TV commentator who spotlighted social problems, promoted left-wing agendas and criticized right-wing positions. Just before the 2006 national elections she joined social-democrat Amir Peretz's Labor party list and got elected to the Knesset. Prior to her career change, Israel's Media Watch frequently complained about Yichimovitz's biases and demanded that her TV station (Channel Two) give equal time to someone with opposite opinions. But nothing ever came of this effort to achieve better balance. The Israeli media is overwhelmingly leftist. Dissenting opinion is not given equal air time.

Every year, Israel's Media Watch awards prizes to crusading journalists intent on exposing the truth (e.g. Yoav Yitzhak who has recently investigated and documented several of Prime Minister Olmert's questionable, possibly criminal actions) and academic researchers who have studied the media's leftist and even anti-Israel inclinations. In 2005 the *IMW* cited Dr. Oren Meyers, now at Haifa University, for his doctoral research that focused on *"Haolam Hazeh"*, a radical left weekly no longer published. Meyers, who received his doctorate from the Annenberg School of Communication at the University of Pennsylvania, reviewed the media's performance over several decades and concluded that Israel's print and electronic media moguls and personalities are essentially opinion molders favoring leftist and even extreme leftist viewpoints. They are not in the business of presenting facts or encouraging objective public debate about issues and government operations. The intellectual elite that control the media are a select in-group with a pre-conceived political program that often ignores facts and reality. No politician can take an independent or opposing tack without endangering his or her public career. An *IMW* study of Channel Two's 2006 election campaign coverage shows how news items were slanted in Olmert's favor and against Netanyahu. Yoav Yitzhak resigned from his paper, *Maariv*, when it refused to publish his Olmert exposé.

During the 1980s Rabbi Meir Kahane set up the Koch party and was elected to the Knesset on a platform that called for the transfer of Arabs out of Israel to Arab lands and other countries because, in his opinion, Arabs do not recognize Israel's right to sovereignty, are a national danger and support the overall Arab effort to annihilate the Jewish state. The media branded him a racist because of his Jewish chauvinism and barred his access to radio and TV studios. He was ostracized and vilified. The term *kahanism* was coined as a euphemism for racism. Then the governing establishment went a step further by formulating its own definition of racism. Whereas the anthropological definition explains that racism is primarily a **belief** in the innate superiority or inferiority of a particular race or group, the Knesset passed a law against racism which was re-defined as: preaching or taking action against a specific ethnic group. Employing this broader definition, the Knesset outlawed racism and disqualifies any person or party considered racist from Knesset membership. In effect, whenever someone fervently takes a strong anti-Arab position on almost any issue, he or she is likely to be labeled a 'racist' by Arabs and their supporters.

The same accusations of racism were leveled against Rechavam Ze'vi a.k.a. "Gandi" who founded the Moledet party and openly advocated the voluntary transfer of Arabs and strengthening of Jewish settlements throughout the Land of Israel as a step in the right direction toward real peace and security. Since Gandi had been a high ranking IDF officer and an expert on counter-terrorism, he was not discredited and persecuted in the media to the same degree as was Kahane. Both men were subsequently assassinated by Arabs.

Interestingly, the media never alludes to Arab oppression of Jews, Copts, Druze or Christian groups as racism. Reports of attacks on Jews in Yemen, Tunisia and Morocco are not seen as racist actions. Arab anti-Semitism in their literature and TV programming is a serious problem but is hardly covered by Israel's media although there are a number of academic institutions that study this phenomenon in depth.

During the 1990s Israel's Media Watch conducted quantitative studies of radio, TV presentations and newspaper coverage. These studies show that far more air time and print space was given to leftist spokespeople. This predisposition to favor leftists continues to this very day. When a TV news presenter has two respondents in the studio, he or she will almost invariably turn to the leftist first. The right-wing representative then has to react instead of being free to present his views as he had planned. I have often tuned into radio programs where the announcer gave the leftist interviewee ten to fifteen minutes of uninterrupted free time to expound his opinions. This never happens when the interviewee is a nationalist or religious leader or advocates a vigorous policy in response to Arab aggression be it military, political, economic or ideological. Spokespersons with nationalistic views not acceptable to TV and radio hosts are constantly interrupted and not allowed to fully elaborate upon their explanations.

In the summer of 1995 I attended a now famous mass rally in Jerusalem organized by the Likud and others then in opposition to Prime Minister Rabin's "peace process" that had led to a steep increase in Arab terror attacks and loss of lives. Avishai Raviv, a Shin Bet secret service agent-provocateur who was also a confident of Yigal Amir (later convicted of assassinating Rabin) composed photo-montage posters of Rabin in a Nazi SS uniform and placed them strategically in line with the TV cameras to create the false impression that the rightist opposition was extreme and dangerous.

Avishai Raviv and Israel's Shin Bet secret service in cahoots with Israel public TV also staged a purported secret meeting of a supposedly clandestine right-wing underground organization called Eyal. I saw this televised on the evening news and assumed that this was real. It later transpired that Eyal was created by Avishai Raviv and that the whole item was a media fraud perpetrated by Raviv and Eitan Oren, an Israeli TV news producer. As a member of the Israeli media establishment, Oren was later awarded a prize for his deception instead of being fired for his unethical deceit aimed at de-legitimizing those in opposition to deadly appeasement policies.

Singers, comedians and other popular celebrities frequently appear on talk shows if they profess leftist opinions but are pretty much ignored if they sympathize with rightist ideologies. Indeed, *ideology* has become a dirty word for pundits who link it to the settler movement that, as Goren said, is invariably censured. Binyamin Netanyahu and other right-wing figures are almost always hit with tough questions and incessantly interrupted. But when the news prima donnas query left-wing activists it comes across, both on TV and radio, as a chat between buddies who pretty much agree on everything. While anyone coming close to

Kahane's or Gandi's points of view has a poor chance of getting a fair hearing, Arab spokesmen on behalf of the Palestinians such as Sufian Abu-Zaide, frequently get a warm reception in the TV studios. Even hooded as well as bare-faced Hamas spokesmen are seen and heard on Israeli TV. This is, to a large extent, because Arab adversaries and Israel's media share a common language.

When TV and radio super stars chat with Arabs, they talk about "territories" or "Palestinian territories" forgetting that Judea and Samaria constitute the heart of the Jewish homeland. They refer to the "occupation" of these lands conveniently forgetting that Israel has returned to places steeped in Jewish history but until 1967 were, in fact, territories that had been forcibly taken over by Jordan and Egypt. Radio and TV announcers still use the appellation "West Bank" which was/is the Jordanian term for Jew-free Judea and Samaria during the nineteen (1948-1967) years they ruled this area. In 1988 King Hussein relinquished his claim to the "West Bank" even though the resident Arabs were citizens of his kingdom. Despite all this, Israeli commentators still, on occasion, use "West Bank" as if they were employees of Jordanian television.

To help promote their political agenda, Israeli pundits have invented clear-cut identities for the various groups that participate in public affairs. For instance, an Arab resident of Akko, Jaffa or Ramle is an "Israeli Arab" even if, as is often the case, he himself proclaims that he is a Palestinian, identifies with his brethren in "the territories" and supports Fatah or Hamas, if he is very religious. The kings and queens of Israeli radio and TV are invariably surprised whenever an "Israeli Arab" is caught helping Palestinian terrorists by driving them into Tel Aviv and guiding them to their targets. Presenters who are normally able to explain everything cannot comprehend why an Arab with Israeli citizenship who enjoys all the liberties one finds in any modern western country (which is the way these commentators define Israel) would want to take part in devastating attacks against their Jewish neighbors.

Of course, anyone who thinks that there is no separate "Palestinian" identity is not invited to participate in TV and radio programs. No one will be permitted to remind listeners that there is no unique Palestinian language, culture, history or religion. The "Palestinians" are Arabs, speak Arabic, adhere to Islam and conduct themselves as other Arabs do in Iraq, Syria or Jordan. Indeed, one of the fundamental tenants of radical Islam which is now the most dynamic force in the Arab world is that the borders between Iraq, Syria, Lebanon, Morocco and Algeria, etc. are all artificial delineations drawn up and imposed on the Arab world by Christian colonial powers. The Hamas covenant (which they have conveniently translated to English on their website) explicitly asserts that Hamas is part and parcel of the Moslem Brotherhood (founded in Egypt in 1928) and an integral unit in the global jihad struggle now being waged. As far as the fundamentalists are concerned, all Arabs and Moslems constitute one enormous nation and that political boundaries are artificial demarcations that obstruct the unity that Allah so obviously and fervently desires.

The "Palestinian" identity problem has a mirror image in Jordan which is a country that was created in 1922 by imperial Britain after WWI when the League of Nations gave G.B. a mandate to rule over both banks of the Jordan River. There is no distinctive Jordanian language, culture, history or religion. It is said that some sixty-five percent of Jordan's population is "Palestinian". As already noted, "Palestinians" living in the "West Bank" **were** "Jordanians" till 1988. Even King Abdullah II married an Israeli "Palestinian" from Nazareth.

One evening in the mid 1990s I was watching Jordanian TV's English language channel and saw talk show host, Sammy Chouri interviewing Professor Shimon Shamir who was then the Israeli ambassador to Amman, Jordan's capital. (By the way, Jordanian officials strongly object to Israel's preference for *Rabat Ammon* which is the biblical name for this ancient city.) Chouri asked Shamir if he subscribed to the "Jordan is Palestine" postulate. The ambassador was quick with his negative reply because the moment it is admitted that there is no difference between a "Palestinian" and a "Jordanian" (or between Palestine and Jordan), then we have instantly resolved the Middle East's longest and most volatile conflict. Naturally enough, Israeli TV and radio continues to call upon Professor Shamir for his "expert" opinions.

When the Labor government of Rabin and Peres signed the

Declaration of Principles in September, 1993 recognizing the PLO (which we often forget is a roof organization for several terror groups of which Fatah is the largest) and thus bringing Arafat along with tens of thousands of his gang (actually gangs is more accurate) to Gaza and Jericho, the Israeli media instantly called this a "peace process". Now that fifteen years have elapsed, one can say that this dramatic policy reversal has had little or nothing to do with peace and is a lot closer to chaos than process. But Israel's media continue to misuse the magic word "peace" as a code word (like "apple pie" in the US or "civilization" in France or "patria" in Spain). All the "good" guys on TV and radio supported transferring territory and sovereignty (at first they used the term "autonomy") to Arafat and thereby helped him consolidate his totalitarian regime. Those in favor of this "process" referred to themselves as the "peace camp". Anyone who thought or thinks that the "process" is really a subterfuge (Arabs use the term *Trojan horse*) to undermine Israel and eventually destroy it, as called for in the PLO covenant that was never really amended, is labeled "an enemy of peace".

The "peace" agreements created fully autonomous Palestinian enclaves within which over 90% of the Arabs in the "territories" became self-governing under the Palestinian Authority or more accurately fell under the dictatorial rule of Arafat and his confederates. From the very beginning an assortment of armed groups (Force 17, Al-Aksa Brigades, Tanzim, Islamic Jihad, Hamas, Popular Front and others) greatly increased the number and intensity of attacks most of which targeted civilians in markets, buses and restaurants. These attacks are war crimes because they target civilians on purpose. Therefore, they are crimes against humanity but Israeli broadcasters rarely if ever describe them as such. Since 1993 over 1500 Israelis have been murdered but the media explains, unbelievably, that this is the "price of peace".

The media in Israel uses the term "*pigua*" instead of "attack". The word "*pigua*" translates into English as "hit". After an Arab terror attack or "hit", the media always focuses 95% or more of its attention on the victims, their families and the injured and traumatized survivors. Almost no attention is paid to the perpetrators who are no longer "Arabs" nor "Palestinians" but rather "terrorists" (*mechablim* in Hebrew). Amazingly, the Israeli media does not employ the term, *enemy*. It may be hard to believe, but you will never hear an Israeli TV or radio announcer use "enemy" or "Arab enemy". I have seen and heard a Hamas spokesman use "Zionist enemy" on Israeli TV but I have never heard anyone use "Hamas enemy".

In March, 2007 I attended a seminar for graduate students in the Department of International Affairs of the Hebrew University in Jerusalem where Professor Alfred Tovias, the department's head instructed his students to avoid the term *enemy* when referring to Hizbullah. He also told them not to use "**our** soldiers" when talking about IDF units that fought Hizbullah in Lebanon because, in the professor's opinion, students must maintain their "objectivity". News editors and announcers also adhere to this distorted mindset.

The word *victory* as in "Israeli victory" has long since disappeared from TV and radio. Indeed, many guest analysts claim that 'there is no military solution to Israel's predicament' as if it were an incontrovertible fact which it is not. People with recommendations to defeat Israel's enemies are rarely invited to expound their ideas. Highly qualified military analysts like Major General (res.) Yaakov Amidror, an expert on Israel's counter insurgency successes is not taken seriously.

Generally the adjective *extremist* is attached to right-wing thinkers and activists. Only Tali Pachima, who was convicted of substantively aiding Zacharias Zubeidi, the Al-Aksa Brigades commander in Jenin has been called "extremist" as in "extreme leftist". Many leftist sympathize with Pachima and think that her three year sentence for helping an enemy is too harsh. For the media folks, as a rule, anyone with strong nationalistic feelings is an "extremist" but identifying with Palestinians is understandable behavior.

Israel's media long ago adopted Arab/Palestinian terminology to describe the difficult situation that the intellectual/political elite have inflicted on the country. For Israel's media, there are "Palestinians", "occupied territories" and a "peace process". At the onset of this "peace process" the media alluded to the 'legitimate rights of the Palestinian people' and the need for 'self-determination' but I have never heard anyone in any medium discuss the legitimate rights of the Jewish people. On the contrary, the axiom that it is immoral for one nation (Israeli) to rule another (Palestinian) is not worthy of debate. Any analysis of the situation on the ground that refutes this description of the relationship between the two parties is ignored; not brought to the public's attention.

Essentially, Israel has for the most part followed a policy of benign neglect with regard to Arabs within and beyond the "green line", the 1949 cease fire lines that are incorrectly referred to as "borders" by so many commentators. No Israeli Arab would ever dream of moving to the Palestinian territories whereas Arabs in the "territories" make every effort to move into Israel proper. I once heard Khaled Abu Toameh who covers Palestinian affairs for *The Jerusalem Post* contrast the peace, ease of movement and freedom of expression Arabs in the "territories" used to enjoy under Israeli "occupation" with the censorship and oppression visited upon them by Arafat, Abbas and the Palestinian Authority. The June 2007 civil war between Fatah and Hamas in Gaza has, as some Arab journalists have pointed out, brought even more havoc and misery to the Palestinians.

Israel's media coverage of the turbulence in Gaza sympathetically focused on the Fatah fighters and their families who fled for their lives. This was presented as a humanitarian problem despite the fact that these "victims" are sworn enemies and potentially dangerous. In addition, no one raised the possibility of these survivors of the Palestinian civil war finding refuge in Arab lands where they share a common culture, language and religion. A Palestinian going to live in Morocco or Jordan would find it just as easy as a Britisher finds life equally convenient in Australia.

The media's unquestioning acceptance and promotion of the "peace process" along with the supposition that Israel has to disengage from the "territories" and the "Palestinians" brings us to the topic of demography. Basically there are two schools of thought. The pessimistic researchers are led by Professor Sergio della Pergola of the Hebrew University and Professor Arnon Sofer of Haifa University. They claim that Arab birth rates and population growth exceeds the Jewish rates. Therefore, it is imperative to abandon territories containing significantly large numbers of Arabs so as to maintain the Jewish and democratic nature of the Israeli state. The Israeli media and most of the establishment elite have adopted this view and give far less attention to other researchers whose findings challenge this. The AIDRG, American-Israel Demographic Research Group led by Bennett Zimmerman and Roberta Seid have written papers that show that della Pergola's data are inaccurate. For example, della Pergola counted the Arabs residing in east Jerusalem as Israeli Arabs and then again as Palestinians. Israel's population 'time bomb' is a **myth**. Jewish population growth vis-à-vis the Arabs is holding its own and may even improve in the long run thanks in large measure to the chareidi (ultra-orthodox) community which does not practice birth control. This controversy is not tackled in depth because it doesn't fit into the media's preconceptions and agenda.

As a footnote, I attended a lecture by Professor Sofer at the College of Judea and Samaria in 2005. Professor Sofer prefaced his remarks with a comment to the effect that here (before a nationalistic audience) he felt free to say things he would not ordinarily say in Haifa or on TV. Popular professors, personalities and artists have internalized a basic fact of public life: the more one leans to the right or questions leftist assumptions, the less she or he is likely to appear on TV or be telephoned for comments to be shared with a radio audience. This contrasts sharply with the eager acceptance of dubious reports from left-wing organizations such as B'tselem and Peace Now that find fault with government actions and Jewish settlement activities. These pro-Palestinian reports are invariably accepted as factual and given extensive radio and TV coverage.

Another subject not often analyzed by the media is Israeli as well as Arab emigration to Europe and the US. Arab emigration out alongside Jewish immigration to Israel probably alters the demographic balance in Israel's favor but this, as far as I know, has never been investigated in any depth by the men and women who dominate the media.

The most serious problem that the Israeli public has with its media revolves around what is **NOT** seen on TV or discussed in radio programs. For instance, not much time is devoted to

Judaism, Jewish traditions or Israeli accomplishments in science and technology. However, this is minor in comparison to political non-reporting.

MEMRI, the Middle East Media Research Institute (www. memri.org) closely monitors newspapers, TV, radio and web sites throughout the Arab world and Iran. It translates liberal, conservative and fundamentalist Islamic messages into Hebrew, English and other languages on a daily basis. It publicizes extremely valuable, insightful information about Arab current affairs and events in Israel's immediate neighborhood. Yigal Carmon, MEMRI's director told me that he has offered his services to media heads but he was rebuffed. Similarly, the Israeli media-consuming public does not get to hear about the insightful reports produced by MERIA, the Middle East Review of International Affairs (www. meria.idc.ac.il) or the superb articles emanating from the Ariel Center for Policy Research (www.acpr.org.il).

Occasionally, Itamar Marcus, director of the Palestinian Media Watch (www.pmw.org.il) is invited into the TV studios to show shocking segments of ferociously anti-Israel programs aired on Palestinian TV. The startling affect of seeing five and six year old Palestinian children being indoctrinated to hate Jews and Israel, pledging their lives to Allah, and learning to imitate "heroic" suicide bombers cannot always be ignored by Israel's all-powerful media.

The re-settlement of Arab refugees in Arab lands (5.25 million square miles) is a taboo subject. Abolishing UNRWA, the U.N. agency that administers the permanent refugee camps where hundreds of thousands of refugees reside is not discussed. Practically no serious debate can be heard about Israel's national interests nor the alternative peace plans such as Avigdor Lieberman's land exchange idea or various confederation schemes. The only game in town is the defunct "peace process" and the equally unworkable "two-state solution". There does not seem to be any way out of the eternal quagmire known as the Arab-Israeli conflict because alternative or more innovative ideas are not given a fair hearing in the media.

Whenever an independent political leader converts to media-speak and adopts a politically correct format, he or she becomes the darling of the media masters. When Ariel Sharon reversed himself and pushed his disengagement plan, TV's channel 2 pundit, Amnon Avramovitz announced that we (the media) have to protect him like an etrog, the delicate citron used during the Succoth holiday rituals. Criticism of Sharon immediately went into abeyance and his alleged corruption cases dwindled to obscurity.

Likewise, before the 2006 elections, Channel 2 voiced almost no criticism of Olmert and thus covertly helped him and his Kadima party come in first with twenty-nine Knesset seats. It is thought, on the other hand, that Netanyahu has been targeted by the media and will, therefore, find it very difficult to win the next round of elections. This contrasts with the treatment that Ehud Barak, now head of the Labor party and Defense Minister is likely to receive despite his reckless record as prime minister before Sharon.

To sum up, the fate of politicians and the country is in the hands of the media commanders who are wedded to an ideology that leans over backwards to appease Arabs, finds fault with Israeli patriotism and denigrates nationalist aspirations. The media is a devoted ally of the intelligentsia that determines right and wrong in Israel. These people have placed themselves on a higher moral plane than ordinary citizens. No amount of objective facts and logic can dissuade these opinion setters from their preconceived, untested theories. A war process is called a "peace process", terrorist leaders become "peace partners" and loyal patriotic citizens can be forcefully thrown out of their homes. This phenomenon of a self-appointed elite dictating social and political policies that do more harm than good has been well documented in _The Vision of the Anointed_ (1995). The author, Thomas Sowell, a senior fellow at the Hoover Institution and former UCLA economics professor, shows how the well-intentioned liberal establishment in America has imposed policies and programs over a forty year period that have proved detrimental and wasteful. Sowell's insights are equally applicable to Israel's problems, which, according to the ruling aristocracy and media pundits, can be solved by dialogues, appeasement and more appeasement whenever new Arab demands are enunciated.

Similarly, Kenneth Levin in his excellent book, _The Oslo Syndrome, Delusions of a People Under Siege_, clearly shows how the left-wing establishment in Israel has dominated foreign policy and actions over a long period. These "thinkers" have brought about a situation where terror groups are ensconced in south Lebanon, Judea, Samaria and Gaza. Furthermore, more and more people (including a few Israelis) are calling for Israel's dissolution. However, the "peace camp" is convinced that their policy suppositions (i.e. Arabs are just like us; desire peace, are willing to compromise, honor commitments, respect other people's religions and support a two-state solution to the Arab-Israeli conflict) are correct. Rarely are they willing to re-examine their assumptions and take an objective look at the Arab world that surrounds them. But this is what we will do in the next chapter.

7
MIDDLE EAST EPICENTER

Perhaps the most common expression one hears when two Israelis bump into one another is: "Ma Hamatsav?" meaning 'What's the situation?' 'Situation' is a one word summation of Israel's problems of which external pressures are, unquestionably, the most significant. To answer this query with some degree of precision one must relate (1) to the Arab world as a whole, (2) to Arab cultural values and (3) to the rise of Islamic fundamentalists and their jihads. All three components profoundly affect life in Israel. Additionally, as government spokespersons frequently remind us, European and American coercion also influences Israeli decision makers. However, Arab world machinations are the primary source of anxiety in Israel. What Arab leaders say and do cannot be ignored. Direct and indirect Arab actions often determine the national mood.

Arab states in their diplomatic activities keep busy jockeying for advantageous positions vis-à-vis their neighbors. Syria, for instance, plays host to terror organizations that have carried out attacks in Israel, Lebanon and Jordan. Indeed, the internal political struggle in Lebanon is greatly influenced by Syria and its ally Iran.

Egypt has the largest and most modern military machine in the Middle East. It also has a treaty of peace with Israel. If, however, the Moslem Brotherhood deposes the Mubarak regime and draws closer to Syria and Iran, then Israel will be in grave danger. In short, the unpredictable geo-political situation can change rather suddenly to Israel's detriment.

The internal situation in neighboring Arab states has a direct impact on Israel. For instance, Hizbullah guerillas attack northern Israel from Lebanon with the moral support of the Beirut government which apparently does not have the desire or power to disarm them. Hizbullah does not request permission to launch raids nor does it respect Lebanese government decisions in this regard. It is now feared that Hizbullah may actually form the next government in Beirut.

In Syria, Law No. 49 promulgated in 1981 outlaws the Moslem Brotherhood. Anyone convicted of being a member of the Brotherhood can be executed.

For Syria, having Israel as its arch-enemy is more advantageous than entering into a peace agreement with it. For over thirty years now Syria has been and still is governed under emergency regulations that justify the complete absence of civil liberties. The Assad regime is able to perpetuate its dictatorship because of Israel. Syria is in no hurry to talk to Israel because the Golan Heights represent just one half of one percent of Syrian territory. A Syria at peace with Israel would have to fend off demands for political liberalization which would probably bring an end to the Ba'athist party's control.

The Jordanian monarchy is really a Hashemite family kingdom. A successful assassination in Amman would probably bring Islamists and radical Palestinians to power. The peace treaty with Israel would become a scrap of paper. The final results of the war in Iraq are also going to seriously affect Jordan and its relations with Israel.

Halim Barakat, a sociology professor who taught at Georgetown University's Center for Contemporary Arab Studies, has written, in his _The Arab World_, that Arab governments do not serve their citizenry. On the contrary, it is the populace that serves the government.

ISRAEL IN REALITY

A recent UN study is highly critical of the Arab world whose progress falls behind East Asia and South America. Not enough resources and little effort are invested in education, social reform, technology and economic development. Most Arab governments are dictatorships that concentrate on protecting themselves while meddling in their neighbors' affairs. The obsession with Zionism, colonialism and 'American imperialism' constitutes a subterfuge to divert attention away from their failure to improve the living standards of ordinary Arabs.

Professor Barry Rubin, director of GLORIA, Global Research in International Affairs Center (Gloria@idc.ac.il) and author of numerous insightful books about Syria and other Middle East countries delivered a lecture in Jerusalem on September 29, 2007. He linked Arab economic and social progress failures with their fixation on Israel. Free speech, criticism and dissent within Arab societies would undermine the war effort against Israel. Spending money on infrastructures and development would divert funds from the war effort. Admitting that the Arab world actually faces more serious challenges than the Israeli "threat" would require diverting attention to these problems. Rubin also pointed out that concentrating on Israel as a mortal enemy is the primary basis that underlies the traditional competition between, Egypt, Syria and Iraq to unite and lead the entire Arab world.

Israel definitely has a problem with instability in the Arab world. How do you achieve peace with nations (all members of the Arab League) that easily break off diplomatic relations with one another and occasionally attack their neighbors (i.e. Iraq-Kuwait, Morocco-Algeria, Egypt-Yemen)? Arab governments make use of clandestine groups to carry out covert operations in sister states and then deny any involvement in the attacks. The massive explosions at the Israeli embassy and Jewish community headquarters in Buenos Aires are examples of incognito terror warfare. The Syrian intelligence services are believed to be responsible for a series of political assassinations in Lebanon including the murder of the former Prime Minister, Rafiq Al-Hariri. More recently, the Syrians are accused of backing Fatah al Islam in its battles with the Lebanese army. The Saudis are building a security fence along their border with Yemen to prevent terrorist incursions. They are also a major source of funds for many Islamic groups including Hamas. Furthermore, substantial numbers of Sunni fighters who target US forces in Iraq come from Saudi Arabia which suppresses its Shi'ite minority.

In addition, dissenting groups in many countries threaten the political leadership and strive to change the social character of the nation. Al-Qaida wants to move the ultra-conservative Saudis even closer to pure Islam. The Egyptian Moslem Brotherhood is a potential replacement for Hosni Mubarak's secular regime. Iraq, of course, is in a state of civil war and the Palestinians now have two governments; one (Islamic) in Gaza City and the other (secular) in Ramallah. It is estimated that the ongoing Algerian civil war has claimed over one hundred thousand lives. But as Joseph Farah, author, journalist and CEO of World Net Daily points out in a July 2007 article about the fighting in the Nahr al Bared Palestinian refugee camp in northern Lebanon, Arabs killing Arabs is not news.

Given all these intra-Arab machinations and intrigues, one can only conclude that no peace process has a chance of success until there is tranquility in the Arab world itself. However, an even greater obstacle to moving the current "peace process" forward is the very nature of Arab cultural norms and values.

The preeminent Arab value is honor. Winning a war brings honor while losing is a disgrace. When, after 1967, Israel found itself in possession of Judea, Samaria and Gaza, it also acquired some two million Arab residents in these territories. I was a newcomer back then but clearly remember Israel Galili, a leading Labor party politico assert that Israel must provide full employment for these Arabs so they will be content and not rise up in revolt. Galili failed to take the Arab notion of honor into consideration. No amount of financial reward can reverse a defeat which is in effect a dishonor. After the September 2000 Al Aksa aggression began, one media commentator offered Gaza Arabs this bit of advice: Stop the violence, open up beach resorts and get rich from the large number of Israelis who will flock to your hotels and restaurants. Ze'ev Galili, a veteran journalist who wrote a weekly column in *Makor Rishon* retorted and explained that Arabs in Gaza have no desire to serve Israelis. They live to undo their 1948 and 1967 defeats and return to Jaffa and Haifa. To suggest that they wait on Israelis in the name of peace and financial security is the ultimate insult.

Revenge is also central to the Arab psyche. An affront must be redressed. Many of the suicide bombers (We should really call them 'human sacrifice bombs' because they don't think of themselves as committing suicide.) who have been apprehended before reaching their targets have said that they intended to revenge a brother or cousin who had been killed or wounded by Israeli security forces in previous incidents. Anat Berko, the author of _Path To Paradise: The Inner World of Suicide Bombers and their Dispatchers_ interviewed female suicide bombers who were caught by Israeli security personnel before they got to their targets to blow themselves up and killing as many Israelis as possible. These women, now in Israeli prisons, think of themselves as <u>failures</u>. They failed to achieve martyrdom which would have brought much honor to themselves and their families. Many streets and squares in Palestinian cities are named for "successful" martyrs. Berko adds that women in patriarchal Palestinian society can realize equality with men only through martyrdom. A martyr goes straight to heaven where she gets to choose her own husband; not a common occurrence down here on earth.

As an aside, I recall interviewing an Arab girl of about twenty-four in my capacity as an employment counselor. She told me that her father had divorced his wife some ten years before and she was assigned to take care of her siblings. (Children remain with their fathers in Islamic societies.) Now the children are older and capable of looking after themselves so her father decided to send her out to work to augment the family income. This young woman like the vast majority of Arab females is a faithful subordinate.

Palestinian education in general and TV programming in particular, as well documented by the Palestinian Media Watch, emphasizes revenge and indoctrinates children to make sacrifices and be prepared for martyrdom. Martyrs are heroes.

The desire for martyrdom goes hand in hand with hate. Back in the early 1980s CBS's *60 Minutes* sent Make Wallace to the Syrian side of the Israel-Syria border where he interviewed a Syrian woman as they both looked over the border into Israel. At one point she said it very simply: "I hate them". Much Arab TV programming and writing about Israel, as translated by MEMRI and similar media watch organizations, contain incitement to hate. Professor Mordecai Kedar of BESA (the Begin-Sadat Center for Strategic Studies) at Bar Ilan University delivered a lecture which I attended (May 31, 2007) entitled "Why Do the Islamists Hate the West?" and the answer is because of **what we are and what we do**. Western civilization is perceived as a threat to Islam.

Unfortunately this hate is just below the surface in daily life in Israel. Back in 1988 as a Labor Exchange staff member, I was sent to help organize a job fair in Beit Shemesh. I went from shop to shop to ask owners to take a table at the fair to recruit additional workers. One day I found myself in a conversation with the owner of a carpentry workshop that employed six Arabs from a village near Bethlehem about 45 minutes away. He told me about an exchange he had with one of his workers about the *situation*. He asked his Arab Palestinian employee how he, the Arab, would relate to him if the Arabs had the upper hand and his worker said that he would kill him. Indeed, some Arab workers have, over the years, murdered their Jewish employers.

A recent instance (March 2008) of Arab employee terror was carried out by 25 year old Ala (Omar) Abu Dhaim of east Jerusalem. He worked as a school bus driver for several years before equipping himself with an AK 47 rifle, two hand guns and a knife with which he slaughtered eight students and wounded another twelve at the Mercaz Harav Yeshiva, a renowned Torah institution within easy walking distance of the Knesset in Jerusalem.

At the very onset of the present Intifada in September 2000, Israeli and Palestinian border police still conducted joint patrols along the lines separating Jewish and Arab population concentrations to prevent terror activities and promote co-existence. At the end of one such patrol, the Palestinian "partner" got out of the jeep and simply shot and killed his Israeli counterpart, a young lieutenant, Yossi Tabijah. The Palestinian policeman, Na'al Yassin was eventually caught, tried, convicted and sentenced (April 2008) to thirty years in prison for this cold-blooded murder. This is not a rare example of spontaneous murder. Incidents of this kind occur from time to time.

Open-minded Arab intellectuals interested in modernizing

Arab society point out that Arabs tend to blame others for their own failures. If Arab armies lost in 1967 it was because of the supposed massive aid provided by the US. If the Arab world is underdeveloped, it is because of Western imperialism. Self-examination and self-criticism are not commonplace in the Arab world. Indeed, most Arab regimes do not allow political criticism. In 2007, Syrian students who authored and disseminated criticism of the Assad government via the Internet were given five year prison sentences. Instead of objective introspection, Arabs are more inclined to let their imaginations lead them on. One hears Saudi and other Arab spokesmen claim that Israel wants to rule all the territory between the Nile and the Euphrates. Jews, according to Arabs and others who believe in _The Protocols of the Elders of Zion_ forgery aim to take over the whole world or spread disease throughout the Arab world.

Women in the Arab world are in the same sociological class as children. They remain dependent over their entire lives. A girl is first under her father's control. After she is married off, she becomes her husband's ward. A woman's body must be covered from head to toe. Women are not permitted to work outside the home unless it is absolutely necessary. Daughters of the wealthy elites who have Western educations are exempted from some of these restrictive customs in several of the more progressive Arab countries. But in ultra-conservative Saudi Arabia, women must always be chaperoned. Drivers' licenses until now were not not issued to females in Saudi Arabia. However, there is a new feminist advocacy group that has begun campaigning to change this and now some women are allowed to drive but under stringent restrictions.

Ayaan Hirsi Ali who was born in Somalia and raised in Saudi Arabia and Kenya as a Moslem published _Infidel_ in 2007. This is essentially an autobiography that describes female abuse and suffering under Islam. Ali, who found asylum in the Netherlands and was eventually elected to the Dutch parliament graphically describes how women are oppressed in Moslem lands. She also discusses the film _Submission_ which she helped Theo van Gogh produce as well as his brutal murder by a Moroccan religious fanatic.

Arab women in Israel live in two worlds. Many attend colleges and universities or find employment in government offices, shops and even on TV and radio. But after work, they return home to their traditional conservative culture that limits their freedom to dress as they wish or socialize freely. Furthermore, Arab women in Israel, like their counterparts throughout the Arab world, can become the victims of "honor killings" when they are suspected of dishonoring their families.

After centuries of religious strife, Western nations have adopted secularism and democracy which is based on political compromise. However, in the Arab world there is still little room for compromise. This, apparently, is an aspect of Islamic thought which is the main cornerstone of Arab culture. Indeed, scholars who know Islam well point out that politics and religion are not separate spheres in Islamic societies. Believers accept that Islam is the embodiment of truth. Since Moslems possess the ultimate truth, it follows that they are compelled to create political entities that are based on Islam. Furthermore, Moslems are obligated to export their "truth" over the entire globe. The Saudis and Iranians spend huge sums of money to spread their competing gospels around the world. However, as Ze'ev Maghen of BESA points out, the deep antagonisms between Shi'ism and Sunni Islam does not mean that these two messianic movements are going to cancel each other out. They are, rather, in stiff competition to spread their particular versions of Islam and combat "evil" Western influences (i.e. individualism, secularism, pluralism, science and democracy). The Moslem outreach campaign to disseminate their absolute "truth" within the Islamic world as well as in the rest of the globe is threatened by rational Western thought that encourages critical thinking. The clash of civilizations is very palpable because modern Western values stand in stark contrast to Islamic dogma. Free thinking, atheism, tolerance of other religions as well as woman's liberation movements are anathema to Islam and directly challenge its fundamental monolithic principles.

Jihad is central to Islam's war on the West. The documentary film *Obsession* vividly depicts jihad. This film contains many segments, recorded from Islamic television news coverage and Websites, which clearly show the raw hatred many fundamentalists feel and project to their indoctrinated followers. One has to see the film *Obsession* to begin to understand the men who carried out the London and Madrid bombings.

Another short documentary film, *Fitna* (strife) produced by the Dutch politician Geert Wilders in 2008 takes up this same theme. This film was disseminated via the Web and instantly infuriated Moslems around the world. Alarmed, the Dutch government immediately issued an apology.

Israel is an outpost of Western civilization. Shopping centers, gay pride parades, drug use, hard rock music and enthusiasm for computers and other electronic gadgetry prove that Israel is no different than the US or the UK. Israelis feel that they are Westerners in every way. New fads and fashions arrive instantly from Los Angeles and Paris. In June 2007, kids stood in line to gobble up the latest *Harry Potter* adventure exactly as their counterparts did in London and New York.

Whereas Israel is an object of intense hate for many Arabs, Pakistanis, Malaysians and others, local Arabs ironically live in and enjoy both worlds: traditional Islam and Western modernity. The joke, 'Israel is the best Arab country in the world' is really a statement of fact. Arabs work side by side with Jews, study in the universities, staff the hospitals and frequent night clubs. But they can adopt a strict Moslem lifestyle if they wish. At the top of minarets nowadays there are several loudspeakers that blast out the call to prayer one hour before dawn as a full-volume reminder to the faithful and also to any Jews or Christians who may be in hearing range, which is the case in several Jerusalem neighborhoods.

The prophet Mohammed was, as history tells us, a military leader. After his death the Arabs rapidly conquered large areas in the Mediterranean basin and Middle East. The initial period of Arab expansion was first and foremost a military triumph. When one surveys the Arab world today we see that militarism has not waned. More military men than civilians head Arab states. Vast sums of money are spent on arms and munitions. Arabs are on the warpath in the Sudan, Iraq, Somalia, Lebanon and Algeria. Fighters believe in the righteousness of their cause which they express in terms of Islamic justice. They believe that they will vanquish their enemies so long as they live their lives according to Koranic principles. The Koran cannot be changed; it is immutable. Islam, in fact, has never undergone a reformation. Differences in interpretation do exist but the faithful all adhere to the same five basic precepts. Anyone like Salman Rushdie who holds an unorthodox or liberal view of Islam is likely to be the object of a *fatwa* calling for his execution. Indeed, leaving Islam to join another religion is punishable by death.

There is no separation of church and state in Islam. Sheikhs are simultaneously religious and political leaders. Osama bin Ladin is a sheikh whose religious wisdom is respected by many in the Islamic world. Iran, of course, is ruled by clergymen. Even secular states like Egypt profess that their governments are guided by Islamic principles. To stay in power, Arab rulers generally avoid confrontations with muftis and other senior clerics whose pronouncements greatly influence public opinion.

There is also a long history of relating to Jews in Arab lands with intense derision. Bat Ye'or, in her *Islam and Dhimmitude, Where Civilizations Collide* (2002) goes into great historical detail to describe the inferior status and abuse of Jews and Christians under Islamic rule. So long as Jews and Christians in past eras paid a special tax and submitted to degrading restrictions, they were allowed to dwell among Moslems as second class residents. In Saddam Hussein's Iraq, Jews were barred from the universities. Even today, Jews are not allowed into Saudi Arabia. Jordanian law forbids Jews from buying and owning land. The Palestinian Authority immediately adopted this law when it received autonomy over parts of Judea, Samaria and Gaza under the various Oslo agreements. Palestinians who sell real estate to Jews or are suspected of facilitating Jewish land purchases are summarily executed. As far as I know, no Israeli government has ever raised this violation of human rights with its "peace partners" even though this should be a cardinal issue because it is linked directly to Jewish rights.

The Israeli Supreme Court has ruled in favor of Arab petitioners in many cases involving land and houses thus affirming Arab equality and property rights. Similarly, the Lands Authority and other regulatory agencies seem to be lax with regard to Bedouins commandeering tracts in the Negev, extensive illegal construction of tens of thousands of houses by Arabs all over Israel and Arab land claims that cannot be documented. In July of 2007, an Arab who owns an apartment in the Jewish Pisgat Ze'ev neighborhood in Jerusalem brazenly put up a 'For Sale' sign to which he added "Arabs only". This was an item in the press but my barber, who lives in that neighborhood, said it wasn't true.

Arabs take full advantage of the National Insurance Institute. The mother of Abu Daoud, the terrorist who organized the 1972 Munich massacre of eleven Israeli Olympic athletes applied to the NII for old age benefits because she had Israeli nationality since she was a resident of unified Jerusalem. In 2007, a group of Arabs from Nazareth petitioned the NII for benefits claiming that they were the victims of a terror attack in the Sinai. A year before, this tour group went to Sinai where they filled up three (Egyptian) buses. At one point the (Egyptian) driver of one of the buses went into a tirade against his passengers accusing them of being Israeli flunkies and consorting with the enemy. He then crashed his bus causing severe injuries to many of his riders. These Israeli (Palestinian) Arabs claim that this was an act of terror and they deserve compensation from Israel (but not from Egypt). One newspaper report I read estimates that Arabs, who are only 20% of the population, receive almost 50% of NII payments annually.

When Arabs (with or without Israeli citizenship) talk about the *matsav—situation,* they describe themselves as an oppressed minority. They refer to the creation of the state of Israel as the *Nakba* or catastrophe. This fallacious categorization of their situation has less to do with the reality of living in 'the best Arab country' than with their concept of and thirst for honor, social superiority and grandeur as was the case in the distant past. With access to instantaneous satellite TV and the Internet, Israeli Arabs now identify themselves more and more with the greater, radicalized Arab world.

Militant Islam increasingly influences Arabs (Palestinians) in Israel as it does elsewhere (i.e. Western Europe). Consequently, the *matsav/situation* keeps getting more complicated and precarious. No one, at the present time, seems to have an answer to the question: "MaYiyeh?" (What's going to be?). What can be said is that Israel is a microcosm where one can observe the clash between Islam and modernity being played out. This is why overseas police officials (including Chinese police officers getting ready for the 2008 Olympic games) and foreign security personnel come to learn how Israel copes with terrorism. Similarly, Israeli experts are in great demand as advisers in other countries where they help organize anti-terror defense systems. Israeli academics at BESA and at the Interdisciplinary Center in Herzliya are in the forefront of international efforts to better understand Islamic thinking and the jihad offensive around the world. It appears that this is going to be a long struggle that will require enormous patience, fortitude and perseverance.

Nevertheless, in face to face relations at work and in the markets, ordinary Arabs and Jews can and do act civilly to one another. This is the subject of chapter 8.

The Western/Wailing Wall plaza. Note weeds growing out of the wall, water fountain for ablutions and roof-top guardpost.

Entrance to the Church of the Holy Sepulcher; Christianity's holiest shrine.

Jaffa Gate, entrance to the old city; celebrating forty years of Jerusalem's re-unification.

A well-defended Jewish home in the old city completely surrounded by Arab neighbors.

Arab butcher shop in Jerusalem's old city.

Succoth booths on newly-constructed balconies.

8
ARABS CLOSE-UP

Israel is a de-facto bi-national state because the Arabs, twenty percent of the citizenry, enjoy full cultural autonomy and Arabic is an official language. Gaza, for all intents and purposes, is an independent entity under Hamas rule and over 90% of the Palestinians in Judea and Samaria are governed (actually misgoverned) by Fatah in the autonomous "A" and "B" zones. Interestingly, whenever the media reports on Jewish-Arab relations they make the assumption that Jews do not understand nor fully appreciate Arabs and their culture. I have never heard a media pundit explore the possibility that it is the Arabs who do not understand or value Jewish culture.

In reality, Jews and Arabs work side by side every day in restaurants, hotels, construction, agriculture, supermarkets, stores, shuks and government offices. It is true that up until the present, Jews and Arabs lived in separate neighborhoods or villages but Arabs have recently started buying apartments in Jerusalem's Jewish neighborhoods in anticipation of a possible re-division of the city. Ordinary Palestinians interested in living normal lives prefer to live under Israeli rule than under a Palestinian government.

I worked in the Jerusalem Labor Exchange which has several Arabs on staff. I always made it a point to discuss current affairs with my Arab co-workers who often surprised me with their comments on the Arab-Israeli conflict. For instance, Yasser Arafat and his cohorts were disparaged. Furthermore, my Arab colleagues were internationally-oriented; sending their children to the US to study and then frequently traveling abroad to visit them. All of my co-workers had close relatives in Jordan and in the Palestinian Authority. We got along splendidly and I never witnessed any antagonisms. I think that this was partly due to the fact that a good number of my Jewish colleagues were born in Arab countries such as Iraq and Morocco and spoke Arabic.

I also observed that my fellow workers as well as oriental Jews in general enjoy Arab music. In fact, Arab-style music (songs with Hebrew lyrics song to Arab-style melodies) is very popular with many Israelis. Wedding celebrations and other festivities often exude an oriental atmosphere that includes hip-swinging dances that are obviously inspired by belly dancing. Indeed, there are belly dancing schools in Israel that are popular with the ladies and routinely attract Russian-born girls although I have not yet discovered the reasons for this attraction.

It should be noted that Israelis socialize with their co-workers to a much greater extent than is the case in America. Therefore, I often found myself at social events and outings with both my Jewish and Arab associates. My work as an employment counselor also brought me into contact with the public that included a significant number of Arab job-seekers. One Arab girl who completed a Ministry of Labor secretarial course refused to work in an Arab office in east Jerusalem claiming that an Arab employer would most likely touch her and thereby compromise her dignity. This girl also told me that her mother had married her father when her mother was just fourteen years of age. She was born a year later and, as a consequence, a sisterly relationship developed between her and her mother. Over the years she helped her mother take care of her younger brothers and sisters.

One handsome young man told a surprising story. Born and raised in Gaza, he found work in Israel, met an Israeli girl, converted to Judaism in order to marry her, served in the Israeli army as a new immigrant (*oleh*) and came to me to see what vocational retraining options were available. Another "Palestinian" visited my office one day. His family name was Kurdi. I asked him how he got his name and he related that his grandfather was a Kurd who had made his way to Jerusalem during the 1940s. On another occasion, around 1994, I interviewed a new immigrant from Iraq. As I took his employment history, I was surprised to learn that he was a Baghdad University graduate. He explained that he was actually a Kurd who had married a Jewish girl. They managed to get out of Iraq to start life anew in Israel. One twenty year old Arab lad from the Old City asked for a referral to our high-level cooking course which required a minimum of ten years of schooling. It turns out that this youngster hardly had any education at all since his father had sent him out to work in restaurant kitchens at a very early age.

I also encountered many Arabs when I served as an IDF liaison officer at the Egyptian border crossings. One day an Israeli Arab businessman from Nazareth passed through our office. He was very upset but relieved to be back in Israel. He had gone to Cairo to buy copper trays, brass trinkets and similar oriental handicraft items that are popular decorations in both Jewish and Arab homes. This shop-keeper's purchases had been confiscated by Egyptian customs officers on the pretext that it is forbidden to take antiquities out of Egypt and he was held on the Egyptian side of the border for three days and then released **without his merchandise**. This incident is illustrative of the problems that Israelis, both Jews and Arabs, encounter in Egypt. Israelis have been attacked and killed in Egypt. More than once, European tourists, mistaken for Israelis, have been similarly attacked and killed by Islamic terrorists called "militants" by politically correct media outlets.

Azam Azam, an Israeli Druze who worked for a textile company that operated a factory in Egypt (to strengthen people-to-people ties) was tried on charges based on superficial, circumstantial evidence and convicted of espionage even though the government and Azam himself denied any wrong doing whatsoever. He was imprisoned for seven years. His release came only after a young Egyptian terrorist, the son of a prominent member of Mubarak's government, was caught in the Negev and quickly exchanged for

Azam. After his release, Azam was welcomed and interviewed several times on TV and generally treated as an Israeli hero that I think he really is.

Large numbers of Druze and Arabs who have been born and raised in Israel do, to a great extent, identify as Israelis. Most speak perfect Hebrew and some individuals can express themselves in superior Hebrew, far above the colloquial level. There are also Arab authors who write in Hebrew. Sayed Kashua, for example, is an Arab who writes for *Haaretz* and has published two novels, <u>*Arabs Dancing*</u> and <u>*Let It Be Morning*</u>. These novels explore the intricate Jewish-Arab relationship within Israeli society. Sayed Kashua was interviewed on Israeli radio (July 27, 2004). He said that he was fascinated by the social and cultural complexities of the Jewish-Arab relationship. Kashua also stated, to my surprise, that he **preferred** to write in Hebrew.

One young man who worked for a while as a security guard in my office after he completed his army service had a Bedouin father and a Jewish mother. This cheerful ex-border policeman is, therefore, both Moslem and Jewish simultaneously. According to Moslem Shari'a law, children are Moslems if their father is a Moslem. And according to Jewish Halachic law a child is Jewish if he is born of a Jewish mother. This fellow was 100% Israeli and personifies, in the extreme, Arab-Jewish integration in Israel.

On 25 October 2002 *Yedioth Aharonoth* carried the following news item: While walking down a street in Tel Aviv, a young man spotted his motorcycle that had been stolen several months before. The police set up an ambush and arrested the fellow who came to get the bike. The arrested motorcyclist turned out to be twenty-seven year old Karim Kafisha of Nablus, the largest Palestinian city in Samaria. For the previous ten years Kafisha had succeeded in using stolen Israeli ID cards to find employment and rent a one room flat in the big city. At the time of his arrest he was employed as a **security guard** at restaurants. Speaking Hebrew without an accent, this young Arab Palestinian successfully passed for an Israeli to enjoy swinging Tel Aviv, made friends with local girls and helped support his poor family back in Nablus that he occasionally visited.

From time to time the police swoop down on construction sites and arrest Palestinian laborers from the "territories" who don't seem to have a problem crossing into Israel proper despite the 10 billion shekel security fence and many roadblocks.

Several thousand Jewish women have married Arab men and live in Arab towns. Some have converted to Islam while others have not. Most have blended into the Arab sector and their children are raised as Moslem Arabs. Sometimes, Jewish women who regret their move try to extricate themselves from their difficult predicament. There is a voluntary organization that covertly assists these women by hiding them from their angry husbands who do not readily accept this kind of rebellious behavior.

The total Israeli Arab population has also been increased by the government's "family unification" program. Essentially, Israeli Arab women marry "Palestinian" men from the "territories" and then petition the Interior Ministry to grant their spouses permanent residence in Israel. The family unification ruse flies in the face of the Arab patriarchal custom whereby wives normally join their husband's family and live in his village. But one Arab man I took care of at the Labor Exchange actually married a second, much younger, wife from the "territories" to his first wife's displeasure.

Israelis flock in large numbers to Arab restaurants in Abu Ghosh near Jerusalem, Jaffa, Akko and towns in the Galilee. Business is brisk, especially on Saturdays. Here then is another venue where Jews and Arabs interact. Similarly, Jerusalem's downtown commercial district as well as my neighborhood shopping center attracts Arabs from nearby. Before the first and second Intifada hostilities, Jewish bargain hunters frequented the Arab shuks in the Old City in large numbers.

"*Time*" magazine did a piece on the Mt. Scopus Hadassah hospital where about half the patients and a good percentage of the medical staff are Arab. The article praised the exceptionally amiable relations that prevail in the hospital which is situated between Jewish and Arab neighborhoods. Like most Israeli hospitals, Hadassah has a helicopter pad to receive casualties of the Arab-Israeli conflict.

The Israeli-Arab interrelationship is paradoxical. In every day life, Jews and Arabs work together, buy and sell from one another and, as in Lod, Ramle and increasingly in Jerusalem, live next door to one another. However, there is an ongoing Arab-Israeli conflict that cannot be ignored. You could say that Israel is a country at peace, yet under constant attack but you can reverse yourself and say that Israel is a country at war albeit with a peaceful lifestyle. No matter what you say, reality at the grass-roots level can prove disorienting because it is so paradoxical. In the next chapter we take a look at these ironies and contradictions.

9
SURPRISES AND CONTRADICTIONS

Sometimes, in polite conversation with friends about the latest misdeeds of politicians and other manipulators, one hears the lament: 'If only Israel were a normal country...' we would not be grappling with the problems that plague us. Surprising things happen all the time: wars break out, general strikes erupt, the Prime Minister and several other leading officials are under police investigation, successful start-up companies are sold for hundreds of millions of dollars and banks declare huge annual profits far in excess of any other sector of the economy and their CEOs are paid fantastic salaries.

After thirty-eight years, expecting the unexpected is a central feature of my mentality. For example, as a Labor Exchange job counselor I visited the lovely Jerusalem Botanical Gardens one day and asked the director if he needed more workers. He said that he was not hiring anyone because, to my surprise, he explained that he always had enough volunteers from England who enjoyed doing basic gardening tasks without pay.

The late, great Yiddish comedian, Shimon Dzigan did a routine in which he proves that he is the only person in Israel who actually works. First he reminds his audience that there is a total population of 3,000.000 Israelis (around 1970). One million infants, children and university students don't work. Five hundred thousand men and women are in the military standing guard. Another five hundred thousand are studying in yeshiva religious academies and they don't work either. An additional 500,000 have government positions in a huge bureaucracy. They do nothing but drink tea all day. This leaves 499,998 people who are disabled or too old to work or are collecting unemployment benefits. So we are left with just two individuals; Dzigan and his wife. Dzigan's punch line is: "I know my wife doesn't work, so that leaves only me. I am the only person in the whole country who works".

The famous humorist, Ephraim Kishon published many books and plays in which he focused on the paradoxes of life in Israel. Kishon noted that Israel is a country 'where the rich vote for socialists and the poor vote for capitalists'. He also pointed out that 'if you hate the politicians, clerks, taxes, the poor services and the weather – it proves that you love the country'.

Contradictions are so commonplace that I normally fail to notice them. For example, newscasters reading the news every hour on the hour will toss out an oxymoron like: 'A **top secret** document discloses that...' The discussion of "secret" documents and meetings on TV and radio programs is quite standard.

Even the Dead Sea is no longer dead. A news item a few years back reported that a certain bacteria had been discovered **alive** at the bottom of the Dead Sea.

Israel has not one but two chief rabbis. One leads the Sephardic-oriental community while the other coordinates Ashkenazi-European interests. Once they had a disagreement regarding the weeds that were growing out of the crevices between the huge stones of the Western (Wailing) Wall. One was in favor of uprooting these plants while the other objected. The weeds have been allowed to continue to grow and add a bit of color to the holy rampart. However, the tiny bits of paper upon which visitors write their personal prayers are occasionally removed from the crevices so others can insert their supplications.

Whenever the cost of "free" public education comes up, a news reporter will invariably find an irate parent to interview. "Free" education in Israel can cost over a thousand shekels a year because parents have to buy books, supplies and school bags, pay for field trips and frequently enroll their children in extra-curricular activities and, if necessary, hire tutors to help in English and arithmetic, two key subjects.

Although the Ministry of Education suggests that 250.shekels ($60.) should be the upper limit that a graduating high school senior should be asked to pay to attend his class' graduation celebration, the wealthy youngsters in Herzliya (according to a radio report on 25 May 2003) assessed 650.shekels ($150.) because they had decided on a fancy dress ball with elegant gourmet food. Israel has definitely come a long way since the austere 1950s when kids had hardly any cash to spend and most were nourished on basic foods.

With people from all over the world, a bewildering array of foreign practices has taken root. For instance, there are professional flamenco dancers who are as good as the Spanish originals. There are also youngsters, mainly from the former Soviet Union, who learn ballroom dancing and go on to compete in dancing competitions.

Rude football fans have run amuck in soccer stadiums as if they were British football hooligans. There is always a sizable police presence at soccer matches just like in Europe.

You can watch your favorite American and British TV programs in their Israeli adaptations. Israel's "A Star is Born" is a reasonable facsimile of "American Idol". The British "Code Breakers" served as an inspiration for "Hatsofen". My wife likes to watch Israel's "Meet the Press" which follows the US format precisely.

Although Israel is, in principle, a Jewish state, little telecast time is devoted to Jewish themes and current events. The situation on the radio is much better because the first radio channel as well as smaller private stations run by people affiliated with religious organizations broadcast quite a bit of Jewish-content material.

The religious public supports its own art and musical subculture that bifurcates into Ashkenazi and Sephardic components. Avraham Freed is a popular Chasidic soul singer who draws big crowds. In August 2007 he appeared in the *Teddy* (Kollek) football stadium in Jerusalem but some ultra-orthodox spiritual leaders forbade their followers from attending because men and women were seated in close proximity to one another; disregarding the traditional separation of the sexes in public places. The concert was, nevertheless, a success.

Religious Sephardim and Ashkenazim too are enthusiastic consumers of traditional Jewish music. The modern orthodox and chareidi communities are not served by the secular media. They prefer vocalists and musicians who perform in a variety of Jewish musical styles: Klezmer, Ladino, cantorial and Rabbi Shlomo Carlebach soul music that appeals to many young people. The Diaspora Yeshiva has a **rock band** whose leader, Avraham Rosenblum is known as the "father of Jewish rock-n-roll". This hybrid music inspires *ba'alei t'shuva*, unconnected or alienated secular Jewish youth who are interested in returning to their Jewish heritage and adopting a religious lifestyle.

Although the Yiddish language is slowly fading away, there is a Yiddish theater group that presents Yiddish plays with simultaneous translation into Hebrew.

There are innumerable organizations that are based on countries of origin. These are fraternal associations of people who immigrated from Britain, Morocco, Iraq, Kurdistan, Ethiopia and France to name just a few. Almost every national-origin group has its own brotherhood. The Iraqis (i.e. Jews of Iraqi birth) operate a museum in Yehud whose displays depict life in Iraq before the Jews were forced to leave en masse. The Sephardic association organizes conventions, lectures and Ladino song concerts. The Association of Former Residents of China in Israel (there is a sister group in Los Angeles) has its own community center, Beit-Ponve in Tel Aviv where they entertain visiting Chinese scholars and Chinese Embassy officials. Members of this fraternal group organize trips back to Shanghai and Harbin, cities that once hosted large Jewish communities before the Communist take-over in 1949. These Jews are mainly of Russian extraction or escapees from Nazi persecution. They now provide scholarships to needy Chinese students who attend Israeli universities.

Just as many Americans proudly describe themselves as "Italian-American" or "Irish-American", almost every Israeli, even native-born *sabras* relates to himself and his fellow Israelis as "Moroccans", "Persians", "French", "English", "American" or "whatever". New immigrants point out, ironically, that back in Russia or Tunisia or Argentina, they were Jews but now in Israel they are identified as Russians or Tunisians or Argentineans. It seems that most people have adjusted to their dual identities; it is part of being an Israeli.

Life in Israel is stimulating because every day brings new surprises. One day I bought a book and as a bonus I was offered an impressive panoramic photo of Jerusalem for another two shekels (60 cents). When I got home and more carefully examined the photo I discovered that it had been printed in Italy even though Jerusalem has a large number of high quality printing shops. On another occasion I looked at the TV program listings in one newspaper and found that a Woody Allen film was going to be shown at 9:30 p.m. By chance I checked a second newspaper and according to their TV schedule a Barbara Streisand film was in the offing. As it turned out, the Streisand film was screened. To minimize surprise, I usually check and double-check everything.

The Israeli cinema industry produces numerous films that relate to Israel's many social problems. A good number of films deal with the army and the Palestinian Arabs whose animosity is rarely scrutinized. Films like *Wasted* (2007) depict military life from a negative perspective. It is almost always the films that present Israeli soldiers as dupes or villains or sadists that are awarded top prizes at European film festivals. Even Israeli film festivals bend over backwards to award prizes to films that dwell on Palestinian "suffering". For the most part, the Israeli cinema is anti-Israel. But once in a while I am pleasantly surprised by a film that highlights Israel's human side. *Teum Kavanot* (Coordinating Intentions) treats the Yom Kippur War with fair compassion and was received with critical acclaim.

In the evening of 3 July 2003 I tuned into Israel radio's Reshet B' station which presented a one hour review of Internet innovations. The first news item was a report about a handful of immigrants from the former Soviet Union who had created a Nazi, anti-Semitic website **in Israel**. As new *olim*, these Russian immigrants had received Israeli citizenship because they have, in their family backgrounds, a Jewish antecedent. Additionally, as new immigrants the Jewish Agency and the Ministry of Immigrant Absorption paid their way to Israel, supported them for at least six months, and provided Hebrew language instruction and, possibly, computer training since the government does run many retraining courses especially for newcomers.

Then in September 2007 the entire nation was jolted by the arrest of eight neo-Nazi gang members operating out of Petah Tikva. The charges against these tattooed Russian youth included assault, threats, illegal possession of weapons, distributing racist literature and the desecration of two synagogues. Immediately, a debate developed between politicians in favor of restricting immigration to *olim* who really are Jewish and strengthening Zionist education and those who object to changes based on one or two statistically insignificant incidents. Over a million Israelis have come from the Soviet Union since 1989 and it is unfair to judge them by the repulsive behavior of a few who happen to have Jewish grandfathers.

I buy my fresh produce in the shuk where hawkers rarely say "thank you" or anything else when you purchase something. However, if I examine some peaches and then decide **not** to buy them, it is quite likely that the stall's vendor will say, "Be well!" There is another frequently heard exclamation that literally translates into "a waste of time". This expression may indicate that you are **really wasting your time** or it could mean **"great"**, **"super"** or **"wonderful"**. This one expression has **two** very different meanings. I, therefore, have to think carefully before grasping a speaker's intensions. As with any language, one has to be alert to dual usage and even contradictions.

The paramount contradiction in Israel revolves around two profound dualities. Culturally, Israel is at once Oriental and Western. It is also simultaneously a Third World and a First World country. Israel belongs to the Third World because of its pseudo democratic political system, high level of governmental corruption, and enormous income differential between the rich and poor, out-migration, brain drain and more. But it is also a First World player because it has symphony orchestras, superb universities, world-class research facilities, clever inventors, many competitive international companies, high technology entrepreneurs, a supportive social welfare system and more.

Life in Israel is full of both major and minor surprises because I live in the East and in the West as well as in the Third World and in the First World all at once. As a newcomer thirty-five years ago I was given a clue to expect the unexpected. When I went to work for the Ministry of Agriculture's Foreign Training Department, my boss explained that his job was to plan things out but he added **"every plan is a platform for change"**. This popular maxim captures the essence of living in Israel. Put another way, one should never take anything for granted.

If a politician says something today he is likely to say or do the opposite tomorrow. When Yitzhak Rabin campaigned in 1992 for the premiership he emphatically declared "that it is inconceivable that Israel would relinquish the Golan Heights". A year later, after he was elected Prime Minister, he was in contact with the Syrians and reportedly ready to give up the Golan. A decade later Ariel Sharon equated Netzarim (the most isolated Jewish settlement in the very center of the 365 square kilometers Gaza Strip) with Tel Aviv; laws that are applicable in Tel Aviv will also determine Netzarim's fate. Two years later in August of 2005 it was Sharon and his government that expelled the Jews from Gush Katif and destroyed Netzarim. Israeli politicians frequently surprise the public by changing their positions, even on fundamental issues.

It may come as a surprise to learn that a small number of high level Israelis have been tried and convicted of spying, mostly for Russia's KGB. Israel Bar, Shabtai Kalmenowitz, Marcus Klingberg, Shimon Levinson, Udi Adiv and Alexander Radliss are a few of Israel's traitors. A news item on 24 August 2007 reported that Klingberg has admitted that his wife Wanda was also a Soviet agent. More recently, Mordecai Vanunu spent eighteen years in jail for revealing details of the Dimona nuclear research facility. He has joined the Anglican Church and refuses to speak Hebrew.

Even purchasing an apartment from one of Israel's best known construction companies can result in an unpleasant surprise. In 2007 the large Heftsiba Corporation went bankrupt and several hundred families who had paid substantial down payments on flats not yet completed lost hundreds of millions of shekels. Their savings disappeared with Boas Yonah, the CEO who was later arrested in Italy. However the government and banks immediately expressed their intention to intervene and alleviate the buyers' losses.

Prudent Israelis have learned to ask a lot of questions. One also avoids people who guarantee results. One can never categorically assume that a politician or merchant can back up his guarantees. Of course, problems of honesty and loyalty are not unique to Israel. Britain had Kim Philby and the Cambridge spy group that caused tremendous damage to the UK and US intelligence networks and adversely affected Anglo-American cooperation in this sphere. More recently, the guys who ran Enron defrauded American investors out of billions of dollars using all sorts of gimmicks including setting up over eighty phony off-shore companies. _Pump and Dump_ by Robert H. Tilman and Michael L Indergaard explains in detail how some large companies, with the connivance of financial institutions, manipulate stock prices at the expense of small investors in the US.

Israelis live with contradictions and surprises. They can never take anything for granted. Perhaps this explains the popularity of a bumper sticker that appeared right after the Yom Kippur War. It announced, 'God, You Can Rely on Him'. The inference was that you cannot rely on the political and military leadership that failed to respond to the many signals that war was about to break out. Today, many non-religious people use the expression, "With God's help". Indeed, even Arabs interject "With God's Help" in Hebrew and it is fairly common for both Jews and Arabs to use the Arabic equivalent, _Inshallah_.

Daily life in Israel is never boring because it is full of surprises. But these surprises are really quite minor when compared to the fundamental issues that render Israeli society contentious and unstable. The last chapter looks at Israel's complex internal problems.

10
COMPLEXITIES AND COMPLICATIONS

The definition of a Zionist, according to an old joke, is: One Jew raising money from a second Jew to send a third Jew to Israel. On a far more serious plane, the question of 'Who is a Jew?' is a hotly debated issue in Israel. Hillel Halkin, writing in The Jerusalem Post on 22 November 1996, summed up the problem. He explained that traditional orthodox rabbis have a monopoly over conversions. The Conservative and Reform movements want to join this monopoly but, Halkin asks, why not extend the monopoly to any college that declares itself competent to convert gentiles to Judaism who then acquire the right to become Israeli citizens? Halkin observes that someone living in Paris who may be totally alienated from Judaism but has Jewish parents is, according to traditional Jewish law (Halacha), a Jew while somebody else who lives in Israel, speaks Hebrew and serves in the army but **does not** have a Jewish mother is a gentile (with or without Israeli citizenship) as far as the as the Israeli Ministry of the Interior is concerned. Ironically, over one million non-Jewish Arabs **are** Israeli citizens.

There are five interconnected, complex questions here that

coalesce into a most confusing situation that probably has no parallel in the world:

1. Who is a Jew?
2. Should Reform and Conservative conversions be as valid as Orthodox conversions?
3. Who should set conversion standards and administer the conversion process?
4. Who is entitled to Israeli citizenship?
5. Must all Zionists reside in Israel; serve in the army?

The conversion procedure dispute is not a trivial matter because there are over 300,000 non-Jewish individuals most of whom identify with Israel and the Jewish people. Somehow a formula has to be found to allow individuals and the state to more clearly define both Jewish and Israeli identities in such a way as to minimize contradictions for the people concerned. At the same time, the link between Jewish history and Judaism on the one hand and the state of Israel on the other has to be kept strong. The conversion controversy has a direct impact on this existential problem. To tackle this issue, a committee has been set up under the chairmanship of Chief Sephardic Rabbi Shlomo Amar to find ways to expedite the conversion process so as to bring more people into the Jewish fold and thereby increase Israel's overall Jewish population and, at the same time, to clarify personal status/identity confusion on the individual level.

Also, secular and religious Israelis relate to the state rather differently; according to the way they practice or disregard Judaism. Secular Israelis see themselves primarily as members of an ethnic group defined by modern Israeli culture whereas orthodox-observant Jews are members in a belief-based religious community that features ritual participation (daily prayers, synagogue attendance and much more). Indeed, traditional Judaism is a lifestyle that prescribes how to dress, when to rest (on the Sabbath), how much money one donates to charity, whom one can marry and how to act properly in just about every conceivable situation. For the religious, there are 613 *mitzvoth* (good deeds) obligations: living in the Land of Israel is one of them.

Essentially, there are at least five Israeli identities: secular-Jewish, religious-Jewish, non-Jewish, Arab-Palestinian and Druze (some of whom emphasize their Israeli identification while others claim to belong to the Arab-Palestinian cultural milieu). All of these divergent Israelis live together in the Jewish national homeland. Despite centrifugal forces, the nation is held together by a variety of shared culture conventions.

The primary language is, of course, Hebrew. National holidays are, for the most part, Jewish holidays. Saturday is the official day of rest. On Succoth (Tabernacle) almost everyone in my neighborhood builds a succa (traditional booth) in which meals are eaten as a way of commemorating the Israelites' forty year sojourn in the Sinai. On Passover, almost all the food sold or served is certified 'kosher for Passover'. On Saturdays, neighborhoods with a predominantly religious populace are blocked off and motor vehicle traffic is prohibited. An *arev* (wire) boundary is strung on poles around ultra-orthodox areas so as to allow observant Jews to carry things on the Sabbath so long as they stay within the *arev* boundary. Marriage, divorce, circumcision, funeral rites and kashrus certification are administered by the religious authorities that are part of the governmental apparatus.

Arabic is an official language and all religions enjoy complete freedom of worship. In fact, the Shari'a law pertaining to the personal status of Moslems is recognized. All Israeli institutions and the bureaucracy are pledged to act in a non-discriminatory manner with regard to every citizen on an individual basis. There are Arab judges and foreign service officers as well as TV and radio personalities.

The Israeli-Arab populace has full cultural autonomy. Arab towns and villages are run by their own locally elected officials. Many government offices (e.g. Labor Exchanges and the National Insurance Institute) in Arab and Druze population centers are staffed by local people.

In the Jewish sector it is customary for every home and public buildings as well to have a *mezuzah* affixed to its doorposts. Observant Jews, upon entering a home, extend their right hand to touch the *mezuzah* and then kiss that hand. Inside each *mezuzah* case is a tiny scroll on which the "Hear O Israel" declaration is written and followed by three prayers. Each scroll is handwritten and must be letter perfect. An omitted letter or a distorted one automatically invalidates the entire mezuzah scroll. Once, when I bought a scroll, I asked the salesman what he does with the voided scrolls. He instantly opened a drawer full of nullified scrolls. The *mezuzah* container is not a holy object. There is, however, an entire branch of Judaic art dedicated to creating original and beautiful *mezuzah* cases. A non-governmental agency, Mishmeret Stam, inspects all parchments and its experts certify scrolls "kosher", devoid of imperfections.

Together, the religiously observant communities avail themselves of the services rendered by a large number of religious functionaries: sofrei stam (mezuzah and Torah scribes), rabbis, Talmud teachers, dayanim (religious court pleaders), kashrus inspectors, mohels who perform the circumcisions, ritual slaughterers, matchmakers and women who are in charge of the ritual baths (mikvot) as well as burial society personnel. In addition, cemeteries are maintained and administered. Synagogue personnel include cantors and caretakers. Radio stations like *Kol Chai* in Jerusalem serve the religious communities and air Chasidic prayer music instead of secular tunes.

There is a whole world of Torah study that includes literally thousands of yeshiva academies and kollels for married Talmudists. The religious sector's publishing industry is extensive. Each religious group publishes its own daily or weekly newspaper and there are dozens of free newsletters distributed on Fridays, to be read on the Sabbath at one's leisure.

In addition to educational institutions, there are also cultural organizations, bureaucracies and religious courts that serve both religious and non-observant Israelis. Religious-secular discord (due to disparate lifestyles and worldviews) is not normally seen on the individual level but rather in the context of these institutions and organizations. The secular-religious conflict revolves around many issues. Non-observant Jews are in favor of public transportation on the Sabbath. They advocate changing the law so that shopping malls will be open for business on the Sabbath. There have also been passionate arguments regarding the sale of non-kosher meats in centrally located stores. The orthodox would like to ban non-kosher meat sales altogether but in cities with many non-Jews they are willing to tolerate butcher shops in more remote peripheral neighborhoods. There is also a movement among secular Jews to cremate people who do not wish to be buried according to Jewish tradition and this has raised the ire of orthodox spokesmen who object to this sacrilege.

Religious Zionist education emphasizes Bible study, Land of Israel studies and Jewish thought over the ages. However, the ultra-orthodox concentrate on the Bible, liturgy and Talmud and pretty much ignore modern Zionist studies while minimizing secular subjects. Indeed, some ultra-orthodox groups do not recognize the state. The secular curriculum has, over the years, reduced its attention to Zionism and has even introduced post-Zionist revisionism. Yuli Tamir, a left-wing Minister of Education even directed the teaching about the Nakba (the 1948 establishment of the Israel state as an Arab catastrophe). The advocates of the various divergent ideologies (socialists, Zionists, anti-Zionist orthodox, etc.) promote their particular educational curricula and endeavor to curtail public funding of antagonistic or competitive school programs.

According to Jewish law a woman cannot become a divorcee unless her husband gives her a *get* (release). Sometimes, the wives of obstinate husbands find themselves in limbo; living separately but not free to remarry because their spouses refuse to grant them a *get*. The rabbinical courts that adhere to traditional Jewish law in divorce matters often fail to bring such cases to a satisfactory conclusion. Many people now demand extensive reforms or the transfer of divorce proceedings to the state's secular court system.

Furthermore, a significant number of secular Israelis can't understand how a modern nation-state can deny its citizens civil marriage. All Jewish weddings in Israel have to be performed by Orthodox rabbis because Conservative and Reform rabbis have no official status. Couples whose partners are of different faiths cannot get married in Israel. Consequently, they are forced to travel abroad, usually to Cyprus which has developed a mini-tourism industry to cater to 'mixed' marriages. These foreign marriages are recognized in Israel for the same reason (i.e. reciprocity) that driver's licenses and various professional credentials are accepted.

It has been forgotten that up to a thousand years ago, Judaism endorsed polygyny (having more than one wife). In fact, in the early years of the state a few Jews from distant central Asian lands, arrived in Israel with more than one wife. More recently, Yaakov Fogelman, a Jerusalemite who runs outreach programs to bring youngsters closer to Judaism and others have reminded us that Rabbenu Gershom's 1,000 year ban has expired and that the state should re-assess its monogamy laws. To date, the issue of how many wives a Jewish man can legally marry has not developed into a controversy in the same way that divorce proceedings have.

Like divorce, conversion to Judaism is, as mentioned before, a highly contentious issue even though the number of converts involved (annually) is relatively small. It arouses strong feelings. Both the Reform and Conservative movements want official recognition for the conversions they perform according to their particular interpretation of Judaism. When a conversion is accepted as valid by the official orthodox authorities, the convert can apply to the Interior Ministry for citizenship. He or she is then at liberty to marry within the Jewish people, or as some humorously say, tribe.

Not only do Israelis have to contend with secular/religious discord and all of the problems surrounding the 'who's a Jew?' issue, but they also have to deal with foreign, non-Jewish groups who take a special interest in the country and are determined to advance their own goals. The average Israeli does not normally come into contact with UN personnel, Vatican representatives, the Jerusalem Moslem Mufti or foreign consuls but these officials are permanent features of the social/political landscape and have to be considered by decision makers. Ordinary Israelis are aware, however, that foreign representatives and activists who promote their own agendas and sometimes undermine Israel's policies and sovereignty also bring into question Israel's legitimacy.

It should be recalled that from 1948 until the early 1990s, the Vatican and many countries like India, China and east European nations refused to have diplomatic relations with Israel. Even today the American Consulate General in east Jerusalem reports directly to Washington and not to the US embassy in Tel Aviv. About twenty years ago, I dropped into the Spanish consulate in west Jerusalem (there is a separate consulate in east Jerusalem) and asked, "What do you do here?" The consul responded with, "We are protecting the holy places." Israel, of course, has been doing a pretty good job of protecting the holy places despite Moslem-Christian friction and Christian-Christian rivalries. Inter-religious belligerence in regard to the holy places is always just below the surface. Yasser Arafat initiated hostilities in 1996 when Olmert (as mayor of Jerusalem) and former Prime Minister Netanyahu opened the fascinating Western Wall tunnel to tourists. Arafat, an Arab born in Egypt, called for attacks on Israeli positions because he negated the Western Wall's holiness for Jews by asserting that Mohammed had tethered his mythical horse, Buraq, to the Wall and so it is actually more holy to Moslems.

Yasser Arafat could say almost anything and the Western media would swallow it as the gospel truth. Andrea Levin, the executive director of CAMERA (Committee for Accuracy in Middle East Reporting in America) writing in *The Jerusalem Post* on January 5, 1996 about Arafat's declaration that Jesus was a Palestinian reviews how the media barely reacted to this patently false assertion. Indeed, over the past twelve years since Levin's essay appeared, the media has paid scant attention to Moslem attacks on and abuse of Christians residing in Bethlehem and neighboring suburbs. In response to Moslem pressures many local Christians have chosen to emigrate. Three thousand Christians in Gaza are desperate to leave after the kidnapping and murder of 26 year old Rami Iyad on October 6, 2007 by unknown assailants; assumed to be Moslem fundamentalists.

Moslem-Christian tensions increased in 2003 when the Moslem leadership started building a new mosque on disputed land adjacent to the Basilica of the Annunciation in Nazareth. This mosque was planned to tower over the church. The Israeli government found itself in the middle of this potentially bloody confrontation but acted quickly to bulldoze the foundations and re-establish the status quo.

The Moslem Waqf controls the Temple Mount. Visitors are carefully screened for weapons and bombs but also for prayer books. The Moslem authorities do not allow Christians or Jews to pray on the Temple Mount although this site is holy to all three religions (especially for Jews). Unfortunately, the Israeli government with its secular orientation refrains from interfering in this matter and, in this way, yields to Islamic intolerance. The government has also failed to stop destructive excavations on the Temple Mount that obliterate important archaeological finds before they can be properly studied.

The Church of the Holy Sepulcher is considered to be Christendom's holiest site. The interior of this most ancient church is divided up between the Greek Catholics, Roman Catholics, Armenians and Copts. The roof has been allotted to the poverty-stricken Ethiopian Christians who live in hovels in a side courtyard. From time to time, disputes break out between the church dignitaries over jurisdiction and rights. When this happens, the Israeli government finds itself in the middle of a difficult dilemma.

A similar problem arose during the Greek Orthodox patriarch succession fight that also involved the leasing of a large Church-owned dormitory in the Old City to a Jewish organization. This transaction greatly irritated most of the pro-Palestinian Church fathers who deposed the offending patriarch.

Arabs also take pot shots at Jews who go to pray at Rachel's tomb near Bethlehem and Joseph's tomb near Shechem (Nablus). When I was a newcomer, I visited Joseph's tomb which was then on the outskirts of Nablus. Today, Nablus city expansion has enveloped this Jewish holy site that Palestinian attackers burnt when they went on the second Intifada warpath in September 2000. Jews traveling to Joseph's tomb to pray or study now require IDF permission and an armed escort.

Just about every Protestant denomination has a foothold in Israel. Most of them identify with the Palestinians but a minority is Zionist and supports Israel. The Quakers are extremely pro-Palestinian and anti-Israel. By contrast, the Baptists operate a 'Baptist Village' near Kfar Saba where some of the Israeli league baseball games are played.

The Baha'i World Center is in Haifa because its founder, the Bahala Ala had to flee from his native Persia (Iran) in the mid nineteenth century. The Baha'i emphasize peace and mankind's universality. They also like to remind people that they are neither

Christians nor Moslems. To their misfortune, since the 1979 Islamic revolution in Iran, Baha'is have been persecuted and killed there.

The Scottish Church in Jerusalem is centrally located and runs a small guest house. They distribute two flyers; one describes the hotel while the other outlines their local history which is slanted in favor of the Palestinians and against Israel. For instance, the history flyer states that they were caught in the crossfire between Jordanians and Jews during the 1948 War of Independence but they do not explain that the bullet holes in their walls were made by Arab Legion riflemen. They proudly mention that an archaeological excavation on their premises unearthed valuable finds. However, they fail to say that the most valuable of these finds is a small (about 10cm.) silver band, 2,500 years old, on which is inscribed the Priestly Blessings **exactly** as they are recited today in synagogues.

The Presbyterians and Anglicans are very keen on divesting in Israel. They urge companies not to invest in Israel or do business with Israelis. Even the UN, back in 1975 declared that Zionism is racism. It took the UN about thirty years to reverse itself. Over the years a huge number of UN resolutions have unfairly condemned Israel. It is no wonder that Israelis feel that 'the whole world is against us'.

Even supposedly neutral NGOs like Amnesty International are biased against Israel. For example, Amnesty's 2003 report on the Israeli-Palestinian conflict declares that the presence of Israelis over the "green line" (the 1949 cease fire lines) is a war crime. At their news conference attended by David Bedein who taped the briefing, Amnesty International's Israel chairman, Aharon Avitar stated unequivocally that he was against killing Israeli civilians who reside over the "green line" but fully accepted the legitimacy of killing Israeli soldiers operating (i.e. carrying out counter-terrorism missions) in Judea and Samaria. So here we have an Israeli supporting the killing of Israeli soldiers. Bedein, whose report appears in *"Makor Rishon"* (19/09/2003), sent his tape recording to the attorney general who was requested to determine if supporting the killing of Israeli soldiers is a criminal offence. Bedein, an investigative journalist, never received a reply to his enquiry.

Anti-Israel Israelis are almost always leftist and secular. Berel

Wein, who writes a weekly *Jerusalem Post* column, spotlighted this problem in an essay published on December 6, 2002. His concluding remarks are well worth quoting:

> *"It apparently makes no difference that the Left has been proven wrong so many times here – in managing the economy, in creating a stultifying bureaucracy, in taxing people out of their pockets and minds, in building settlements while at the same time decrying their existence, in the Oslo peace-process disaster, at Camp David II and Taba – it still is never wrong. Because it is a religion, a faith, and as such, not subject to self-review and painful examination.*
>
> *Until the Left renounces its "secular revolution", its vituperative words against Judaism and religious Jews, its positive aspects – and there are many - will be overshadowed in my mind by this terrible stain on its body politic."*

The anti-Israel activities of so many "neutral" NGOs has prompted Professor Gerald Steinberg, executive director of *NGO Monitor* (and a lecturer at Bar Ilan University) to create a website (www.ngo-monitor.org) that meticulously scrutinizes the activities and machinations of these organizations. NGO Monitor documents the ways in which NGOs distort the truth and manipulate facts against Israel.

In 1993 Robert D. Kaplan, who writes for *"The Atlantic Monthly"*, published *The Arabists*, a detailed history of American and British missionaries and other expatriates who spent decades in the Middle East and came to appreciate Arab culture and identify with Arab aspirations although they were usually at a loss to understand Arab political and socioeconomic faults. In a chapter that touches on the Arab-Israeli conflict, Kaplan quotes extensively from various American and Anglo Arabists who were well acquainted with both Arabs and Israelis. Kaplan sums up the experiences of these Arabists with the following comments: "Israelis were easy people to respect but difficult people to be around. The problem was they treated you like just another member of their immediate family, without decorum and comfortable distance normally provided to strangers. Moreover, they were just as smart as you, and what was worse, they never let you forget it." (p.121)

American and British Arabists who can lay claim to intellectual honesty and objectivity prefer Arabs and dislike Israelis (and Jews). Hillel Halkin related to this point in an article published in *The Jerusalem Post* on 2 May 2003. Halkin points out that Jews, even in the remotest corners of the globe, stick out and disturb the natives. This is not a matter of anti-Semitism but rather an example of cultural dissonance. Halkin succinctly puts it this way:

> *"...as a people, we have our annoying qualities. In fact, we Jews in Israel complain about ourselves to each other all the time. We're loud. We're pushy. We're tense. We're aggressive. We're nosy. We're argumentative. We're always trying to cut corners, always looking for bargains and ways of outsmarting one another. It's a relief to go abroad and get away from ourselves to places where people are polite and talk quietly and don't haggle and mind their own business.*
>
> *But we also know that, all in all, we're not that bad, and that every one of these traits has its positive side. We're tense? Of course we are; that's what keeps us on our toes. We argue a lot? That's because we're intellectually alive and honest about our opinions and not afraid to let others know we disagree with them. We're nosy? Well, we're curious; our minds are always working, asking questions. We're loud? Yes, and we don't hold back our emotions until we get ulcers, or take to drink, or run amuck in the street and gun down a dozen of our neighbors."*

I wish to add another point Halkin makes. The Swedes, British, Americans and other polite folks around the world emphasize form over substance. You have to spend years among these quiet, reserved, 'mind your own business' people before you become aware of their negative qualities and shortcomings. The opposite holds true of Jewish Israelis. You first find yourself knee-deep in noise, competition, excessive frankness and the invasion of your privacy. Within a month, visitors can list many negative traits. But over the long run, one gets accustomed to the pragmatism and resourcefulness that characterizes Israeli behavior. Despite all the enormous problems with which they have to contend, Israelis are optimistic, friendly, fair and truly international in their openness to the world.

The 2005 Nobel Prize in economic science was awarded to Professor Robert J. Aumann of the Hebrew University's Center for Rationality (along with Thomas C. Schelling of the University of Maryland) for advances in game theory. Professor Aumann belongs to PSI, Professors for a Strong Israel, an organization whose members are drawn primarily from the natural sciences and economics. Interestingly, most left-wing academics come from the humanities and social sciences. After receiving the Nobel Prize, Aumann was a guest lecturer at numerous gatherings in Israel and abroad. I attended his presentation to the Professors for a Strong Israel group. He analyzed Israel's appeasement policies and came to the conclusion that 'peace now' is a delusion. People who believe that peace is almost at hand do not fully take current as well as future adverse developments into consideration. Professor Aumann ended his talk with the observation that it is quite possible that Israel will not survive but he is confident that the Jewish people will endure.

I share Professor Aumann's apprehensions regarding Israel's future because, over the past four decades, I have watched the appeasement process grow. At first, Israel's leaders refused to negotiate with terrorists. Then there was a period when leftists secretly met with PLO representatives. This led to the Oslo declaration which was engineered by Yossi Beilin who Rabin referred to as "Peres' poodle". In 1993 the public was told that we were embarking on a "peace process" which would be founded on autonomy for the Palestinians. Four years later, Yossi Beilin wrote me a letter (dated 13 November 1997) in which he already uses the term "Palestinian state" but declares that in the understandings reached with Abu Mazen no settlements will be evacuated and united Jerusalem will remain the capital of Israel. Today Beilin advocates evacuating Hebron and dividing Jerusalem. Foreign Minister Tzipi Livni believes that it is in Israel's interest to help create a Palestinian state. But I have never heard her discuss the pros and cons of such a development. Given the factual record of the "peace process" to date, the creation of a Palestinian state is suicidal for Israel. Recent history (i.e. the Gaza disengagement), Arab world dynamics (i.e. imminent political leadership changes in Egypt and Syrian support of Hizbullah) and Palestinian terror initiatives (i.e. Kassam rocket attacks on Sderot and drive-by shootings in Samaria) all lead to one logical conclusion: the birth of a Palestinian state will most likely result in an escalation of the Arab-Israeli conflict.

Professor Barry Rubin, in a lecture he delivered on 29 October 2007 at the BESA conference on violence and Islam, looked at the conflict through Palestinian eyes. He made three major points: 1) The Palestinians are trapped by their own ideology to destroy Israel. 2) From the Palestinian perspective, terror actually works. 3) Fatah cannot sign a peace accord with Israel because it is in competition with Hamas; each group tries to prove that it is more radical than its rival.

Israel is a complex country because there are actually five or more Israeli identities. The degree to which Jewish customs, rituals and Torah law is transposed into Israeli culture is highly contentious among the five stereotypes. The presence of many foreign and international bodies further complicates political issues. Also, these alien actors are sometimes in conflict with one another. This is the background for the government's appeasement policies with respect to the fragmented Palestinians who are waging a low-intensity terror war against Israel. No end of hostilities is in sight because, when viewed from the Arab/Palestinian vantage point, they keep making progress by chipping away at Israel's 'red lines' which are constantly moved leftward to accommodate new and more dangerous conditions.

In light of the enormous amount of attention world leaders pay to Israel, it is important to remind friends and foes alike that Israel is a tiny country with few natural resources. The total population is just over seven million and is split along ethnic lines, religious affiliation, incongruent lifestyles and significant economic class differentiation. Looking at Israeli society is analogous to using a camera that has to be focused carefully. When an observer concentrates on Jewish Israelis, she misses the Arabs. When our photographer shops for fashions in Tel Aviv, she is not likely to meet ultra-orthodox ladies or traditional Arab matrons.

When praying at the Western Wall, she is unlikely to encounter members of Israel's Olympic team. In short, there are so many complex facets to life in this wonderful little country that it is virtually impossible to focus clearly on all of them at the same time. Therefore, a truly conscientious photographer/observer uses a wide-angle lens and exposes many rolls of film to come up with as accurate (integrated) an image of this battered but beautiful country as possible.

SELECT BIBLIOGRAPHY

Ali, Ayaan Hirsi, Infidel
  Free Press, New York, 2007

Bat Ye'or, Islam and Dhimmitude: Where Civilizations Collide
  (Translated from the French by Miriam Kochan and
  David Littman)
  Fairleigh Dickinson University Press, Teaneck, N.J. 2002

Barakat, Halim, The Arab World: Society, Culture and State
  University of California Press, Berkeley, 1993

Berko, Anat, Path to Paradise: The Inner World of Suicide
  Bombers and their Dispatchers
  (Translated by Elizabeth Yuval)
  Praeger Security International Greenwood Publishing
  Group, Inc., Westport, Connecticut 2007

Cromer, Gerald, A War Of Words: Political Violence and
  Public Debate in Israel
  Frank Cass Publishers, London, 2004

Gilbert, Martin, Jerusalem in the Twentieth Century
  Chatto & Windus (Random House), London, 1996

Gilman, Sander L., Jewish Self-Hatred: Anti-Semitism and the
  Hidden Language of the Jews
  The Johns Hopkins Press, Baltimore, Maryland, 1986

Gur, Janna, The Book of New Israel Food
  Al Hashulchan Gastronomic Media, Tel Aviv, 2007

Hunter, Edward, Brain Washing in Red China: The Calculated
  Destruction of Men's Minds
  Vanguard Press, New York 1951

Kaplan, Robert D. The Arabists
  The Free Press, New York, 1993

Levin, Kenneth, The Oslo Syndrome: Delusions of a People
  Under Siege
  Smith and Kraus, Inc., Hanover, New Hampshire 2005

Parenti, Michael, Inventing Reality: The Politics of the Mass Media St. Martin's Press, New York 1986

Sowell, Thomas, The Vision of the Anointed: Self-Congratulations as a Basis for Social Policy Basic Books, New York 1995

Tilman, Robert H. and Indergaard, Michael L., Pump and Dump: The Rancid Rules of the New Economy Rutgers University Press, New Brunswick, New Jersey 2005

INDEX

A

Abu Dhaim, Ala – yeshiva massacre perpetrator 76

Abu Toameh, Khaled – journalist 66

Abu Zaide, Sufian – Palestinian activist 62

Agrexco – export company 14

Ahrar al-Jalil Galilee insurgency 49

AIDRG – American-Israel Demographic Research Group 67

Alcalay, Reuben – dictionary author 55

Ali, Ayaan Hirisi – Islamic critic 76

Al-Jazeera television network 57

Amidror, Yaakov – military analyst 65

Amnesty International 109

anti-Semitism 10; Arab 60; Jewish 10

Arab emigration 67; employment 87; family re-unification 91; identification 6; military expansion 79-80; political parties 48-50; schools 31; women 77, 78; workmen 6

Arab states – relationships between 71-73

Arabic Language Academy 48

Arafat, Yasser 49, 50, 64, 107

archaeological excavations 24

Aumann, Robert J. – Nobel Prize recipient 112

Avramovitz, Amnon – TV commentator 69

Azam, Azam – prisoner in Egypt 89

B

Baha'i World Center 108

Balad political party 49

Barak, Ehud 46

Barakat, Halim – author 72

Bat Ye'or – author 16, 80

BBC 7, 21

Bedein, David – journalist 109

Beilin, Yossi – MK 49, 112

Ben-Gurion, David 36, 52

Berko, Anat – author 75

BESA – The Begin-Sadat Center for Strategic Studies 76

Bishara, Azmi 49

B'nei Akiva youth movement 30, 46

B'tselem organization 67

Burg, Avrum 50

C

Chabad organization 31

Chadash political party 48

Chief Rabbis – disagreement 94

Choury, Sammy – Jordan TV host 63

Church of the Holy Sepulcher 108

chutzpah 36

Community Center in Kiryat Shmona 23

INDEX

Printed in the United States
By Bookmasters